A RIVER CAPTURED

A RIVER CAPTURED

The Columbia River Treaty and Catastrophic Change

EILEEN DELEHANTY PEARKES

RMB

RMB | Rocky Mountain Books Ltd.
rmbooks.com
@rmbooks
facebook.com/rmbooks

Cataloguing data available from Library and Archives Canada

ISBN 978-1-77160-178-8 (paperback)
ISBN 978-1-77160-179-5 (electronic)

Printed and bound in Canada by Friesens

Distributed in Canada by Heritage Group Distribution and in the U.S. by Publishers Group West

For information on purchasing bulk quantities of this book, or to obtain media excerpts or invite the author to speak at an event, please visit rmbooks.com and select the "Contact Us" tab.

RMB | Rocky Mountain Books is dedicated to the environment and committed to reducing the destruction of old-growth forests. Our books are produced with respect for the future and consideration for the past.

We acknowledge the financial support of the Government of Canada through the Canada Book Fund and the Canada Council for the Arts, and of the province of British Columbia through the British Columbia Arts Council and the Book Publishing Tax Credit.

*I remember when the river and
the people, we both ran wild.*

—SPOKANE GARRY

This book is for the Columbia River.

Contents

The Landscape of the Upper Columbia River Watershed

- Communities flooded by Dams
- Treaty Dams
- Power Dams

Introduction

The mountain landscape of the upper Columbia River basin brims with the power of flowing water. Water burbles, roars, pools and turns. It transports minerals from high mountaintops to valley floors. It washes nutrients into flood plains. It carries fallen trees like matchsticks. It rolls boulders and scrubs gravels clean. The water cycle begins in winter, with abundant snow that forms mountains of its own, in drifts that soften the granite spires and glisten in the sharp sun during the coldest season. In spring, hundreds and thousands of seasonal and year-round streams go to work, draining their liquid charge down the rocky flanks, transporting newly melted snow to the valley bottoms. The transfer of energy that fills the air during the mountain-melt season is at once effortless and astonishing.

By early summer, the melt has subsided. By midsummer, most of the seasonal streams have gone bone dry. The year-round creeks are sighing rather than roaring. The quiet rhythms of water storage settle in.

When did I notice the reservoirs? I can't really say. A handful of years after I arrived in the region, I looked beneath the surface of the striking beauty and abundant water of the upper Columbia River watershed. What I found surprised me: I live in one of the most intensively developed hydro-power regions in North America. The use of water for electricity has a long history, with one of the earliest hydro-power generators on the continent constructed here in the 1890s. Today, over a dozen major dams and generating stations store and convert water's natural power into electricity, providing 50 per cent of the power used in the entire province of BC. Several dams date to the first great period of hydro-electric development in North America, between 1890 and 1930, when private, corporate interests developed the lower Kootenay River west of Nelson, BC. But the biggest projects – and the most ecologically damaging ones – were constructed between 1964 and 1984 by the BC government, under the auspices of an international agreement with the United States: the Columbia River Treaty. Dams and the treaty are woven tightly into the fibres of our regional identity.

The upper Columbia watershed gives birth to the fourth-largest river in North America.[1] This unique interior rainforest is a womb for abundant winter snow and copious rain in the shoulder seasons. The rest of the Columbia's vast watershed terrain – to the south and west, stretching into the United States – is equally commanding in its variety and scope. The great river links the west slope of the Continental Divide with the Pacific Ocean, encompassing

---

[1] The size of rivers can be measured by length, area of watershed and average discharge/volume. The Columbia earns this status based on discharge/volume.

portions of seven US states and one Canadian province, and forming a land mass roughly equal to the size of France. Its watershed
also contains a dizzying array of ecosystem types – from desert to
rainforest – and hosts a myriad of tributary rivers of various sizes,
lengths and power of their own. The American portion of the river's
2000-kilometre (1,240-mile) run is, like its Canadian cousin, also
intensively developed for hydro-electricity. But it is the Canadian
portion that is wettest and most alive with the water that gives the
Columbia basin its power. North of the international boundary, this
15 per cent of the entire watershed provides up to 40 per cent of the
Columbia's international water volume. In dry years, that share can
climb to 50 per cent.

Since 1964, the Columbia River Treaty has tightly governed the
upper Columbia watershed's river management, with Canada annually providing 15.5 MAF (million acre-feet)[2] of stored snowmelt. The
reasons for this storage are twofold: 1) to make greater, more efficient use of the annual surge of water in creating year-round electricity; and 2) to protect urban and agricultural communities from
the annual flooding that is a natural component of a snow-charged
system. The Columbia River Treaty has long been hailed as a model
of cooperation between two countries, and to a certain extent that
has been true. For several decades now, the treaty has been peacefully implemented by a trans-boundary Permanent Engineering
Board (PEB) that has been remarkably collegial. The treaty's in-built
principle of sharing downstream power benefits between both
countries has resulted in both benefiting economically from the

---

[2] An acre-foot is a water-engineering term to describe volume: the
amount of water that covers an acre of land at a depth of one foot.

hydro-power efficiencies. This shared economic benefit is a principle of fairness built into the life of the treaty, expressed by what is also known as the Canadian Entitlement.

The Canadian Entitlement (CE) lies at the heart of the catastrophic ecological and social change caused by the Columbia River Treaty in Canada. As this close look at treaty history will demonstrate, Canada's interest in maximizing the initial monetary benefits of the CE influenced the design of the system ultimately chosen by the two countries. The Columbia River Treaty's power-producing principles – including the CE – *will continue in perpetuity* unless there is a mutual agreement to make changes. If one side wants to terminate the treaty, it must give ten years' notice, and even then certain provisions would continue after termination.

On the surface, all is well and all will continue to be well for infinite peaceful cooperation between the two countries. But there is always something going on beneath the surface of any body of water. Including, and perhaps most especially, beneath reservoirs.

The second of the two main principles of the treaty's management, flood control, will change. In 1964, the US paid Canada US$64.4-million to protect mostly American urban and agricultural communities from spring flood for 60 years, up to September 16, 2024. After that period, the treaty dictates, the US must first call upon its own reservoir system to provide the flood control it needs, before asking Canada to use its extensive reservoirs in the upper Columbia region for that purpose. It is the finite, 60-year flood control provision in the treaty that has opened the eyes of many people to potential changes in the entire treaty structure. Lots of people are talking about the river now: government officials, water policy experts, academics, engineers, resource managers, and tribal and First Nations leaders on both sides of the boundary, as well as many other residents of the upper Columbia region. The voices of residents – of those whose lives were transformed by the advent of the CRT storage system – form the heart of this story of a river captured.

I had already been following the CRT's history across the upper Columbia landscape for several years before I noticed that the water's calm, controlled surface was being agitated by the possibility of renegotiation. As a cultural historian deeply interested in landscape, I grew even more curious about the system of dams and why they existed. At times, as I studied the history of how the treaty came to be, I felt immersed in an uncontrolled stream swollen by spring snowmelt. I clutched at imagined shoreline branches or exposed roots, trying not to get pulled under by the treaty's serpentine policy details, by its political secrets or by its uncomfortable truths. I will admit to nearly drowning myself in engineering reports, economic valuations, maps of transmission lines, old photos of farms flooded into reservoirs, and headlines filled with a spirit of congratulations about the treaty at last being ratified, or with the careful posturing of government leaders.

I will also admit that I wondered all along why I even wanted to know.

History tells two stories of the Columbia River Treaty. One of a model international agreement of cooperation and mutual advantage between two countries. Another, beneath the surface or largely forgotten, of an ecosystem and a way of life upended by corporate greed and betrayal. The widely praised national and international benefits of CRT water impoundment do not extend to the region that provides them. The landscape is a handmaiden for the whole system of dams, profitable hydro-generation and copious irrigation supply.

The development of water resources in the upper Columbia region offers some universal truths about the North American settler culture. It is not the first story of modern humanity's often paradoxical relationship with the natural world and its resources, nor am I idealistic enough to assume it will be the last. We live in a time when prosperity seems all too dependent upon use and abuse of the resources we hold as a common good. This story exemplifies the short-term view that often governs our choices. As I journeyed from one corner of the upper Columbia basin to another, I learned to ask three questions: *what has changed in the landscape where I live, who changed it, and why?*

Wherever you live, I encourage you to do the same. In the answers to these questions may well lie the key to our future.

Preparing the Ground: Key Events Preceding the Columbia River Treaty

1. Swimming through a River of Sage

It's a hot mid-spring day when I pull into the border crossing at Waneta, BC, on the start of a journey to reclaim the memory of ocean salmon. It's sometimes hard to fathom that ocean fish once swam 2000 kilometres (1,240 miles) inland and upstream, from the mouth at Portland, Oregon, all the way to the Columbia River's headwaters in the Rocky Mountain trench. It seems an impossible journey – to seek a path into the heart of three mountain ranges just west of the Continental Divide, several hundred kilometres from the Pacific Ocean. But it did happen, and for thousands of years. I want to see for myself how and why the fish no longer spawn in the upper Columbia region. I want to understand first-hand, not from maps, not from Google Earth, how the Columbia River and its tributaries descend from the rainforest where I live, into the dry desert where Grand Coulee Dam sits. This was once the path of a remarkable fish.

I sit in my truck, waiting for my turn to cross. Beside me, the Columbia ripples lightly with the water discharged by Waneta Dam, located just above the boundary at the Pend-d'Oreille River confluence.[1] The Columbia will tumble south for less than half a mile before crossing the border between the two countries and meeting the slack water from Lake Roosevelt, Grand Coulee Dam's 200-kilometre-long (125-mile) reservoir. When it's my turn, I show my US passport and am allowed to cross the 49th parallel, that imaginary line that tells me I am in another country. As an American living in Canada since 1985, I have spent much of my adult lifetime negotiating this razor-sharp boundary. My American passport and Canadian permanent resident card allow me to cross the border with a measure of ease, as long as I remain in good standing. Through my fluid passage, I have become painfully aware of the restrictions nationality imposes on anyone's understanding of home and place, and on the freedom of the great Columbia River and its fish.

Glaciers rather than floods shaped the uppermost Columbia basin into a series of valleys and mountain ranges oriented in a north-south direction. The snowmelt makes its way through these long, rugged corridors. The east-west international boundary at the 49th parallel works sharply against the natural geography, confounding the ability to understand the way the rivers flow. In the upper watershed, the Columbia, Kootenay, Pend-d'Oreille, the Kettle, the Flathead, Moyie and Okanagan rivers are all sliced neatly in two by the border.[2] The placement of this boundary, determined by politi-

---

[1] In the US, Pend-d'Oreille is spelled "Pend Oreille"; for simplicity, this book will use the Canadian spelling throughout.

[2] Kootenay is spelled "Kootenai" in the US, and Okanagan is spelled "Okanogan"; this book uses the Canadian spellings.

cians who never visited the region, confounds any understanding of the Columbia River's geography.

Just south of the international boundary, the great Interior Plateau spreads like an open hand across the central interior of Washington State. Fed by the narrow, wet and tightly charged origins of the Columbia's Canadian birthplace, the American Columbia becomes middle-aged with abundance and grandeur as it carves its way south through the plateau. A great glacial flood once formed this flat palm of desert, burnishing the soil's ancient skin with ripples of silt and deep fissures of basalt. Amidst the basalt and ancient silt sits one of the greatest water impoundment stories of the west: Grand Coulee Dam. It is Grand Coulee that blocked the salmon from swimming upstream into Canada. This by-product of the dam – the extirpation of four species of spawning ocean fish – feels more momentous to me than the concrete barrier itself.

I drive south for about an hour along the Lake Roosevelt reservoir before turning in to rest at a National Park Service campground at the former townsite of Marcus, Washington. Prior to becoming a farming community, Marcus was a village of the Arrow Lakes Indians (Sinixt), the tribe whose traditional territory surrounds the main stem of the upper Columbia River from just south of Marcus to the Big Bend of the Columbia, north of Revelstoke, BC. The Sinixt call this place *nts'elts'elitkw* – "trees standing in water," a reference to the annual flood cycles of a Columbia River that sometimes overflowed its banks. Grand Coulee Dam's completion caused a permanent flood over many town sites and ancient indigenous communities, including the Sanpoil, the Spokanes and the Skoyelpi. It seems as if no one has driven down to "trees standing in water" in some time. The asphalt road to the reservoir shoreline is littered with the trees' rusty, cast-off needles. A warm wind tosses the ponderosa pines above my head. I stretch across the seat and, in a few moments, I am asleep.

***

For thousands of years, the upper Columbia basin had no 49th parallel. Home to a group of closely related Salish tribes, the upper basin was segmented only by a loose assembly of cultural boundaries, usually defined or reinforced by geographic features. These barriers in turn gently shaped the refinement of distinct cultures, with various dialects and languages, identities, stories and practices emerging from a deep taproot – the proto-Salish culture that arrived over ten thousand years ago.[3]

The hub of the pre-colonial upper Columbia basin was an immensely productive salmon fishery at a place south of *nts'elts'elitkw* (Marcus), another large village called *sxwenitkw* (Kettle Falls), variously translated as "roaring," "sounding," "swift" or "noisy" water.[4] *Sxwenitkw* was a series of cascading waterfalls on the Columbia where salmon could be harvested as they struggled up the rocky steps in the river. It was a place of trade, harvest and cultural exchange – all centred around the renewable resource of ocean

---

[3] Chance.

[4] Hudson's Bay Company chief trader Angus McDonald came from Scotland in 1838 and for years lived almost exclusively with the Nez Perce, Flathead Salish and Blackfoot Indians at trade posts in present-day Idaho and Montana before assuming the post of chief trader at Fort Colvile in 1838. Fluent in several tribal languages as well as Gaelic and English, McDonald called the river "Sounding Waters." He observed salmon crowded so thickly in the "billows at the foot of the falls" that he commented they might have just as easily been speared with a rifle. It is McDonald's translation of the term *sxwenitkw* that I use here, with respect to all other variations.

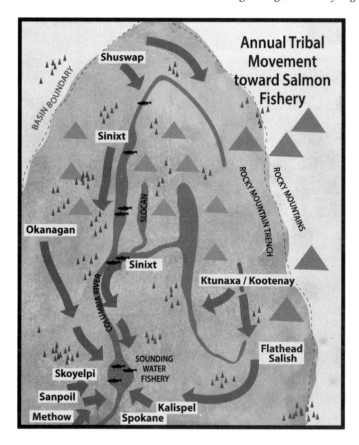

The Upper Columbia Drainage Pattern is primarily north-south, with the interior Salish, Sinixt and Okanagan, and the Ktunaxa/ Kootenai moving freely up and down the Okanagan and Columbia River valleys and the Rocky Mountain Trench. At the northern tip of the upper Basin lived another Interior Salish tribe, the Shuswap.

MAP BY PINK DOG DESIGNS AND COURTESY OF TOUCHSTONES NELSON MUSEUM OF ART AND HISTORY.

fish returning annually to spawn. Contemporary archaeological evidence points to tribal use of the fishery dating back more than 9,000 years.[5] Three species of ocean salmon (chinook, sockeye and coho), and steelhead trout all passed through here on their journey upstream to spawning grounds in the wet, cool mountains. Resident fish abounded, too, with over a dozen species available for harvest.[6] The abundance of the river's fishery and its cultural significance is well documented. In large part due to this resource, the British fur trade activities initiated near the mouth of the Spokane River[7] eventually moved to focus on the area around the great falls, with the Hudson's Bay Company establishing a permanent fort at Sounding Waters in 1825.[8]

The great salmon fishery formed a hub in an indigenous wheel that extended east to the Rocky Mountains, west to the Okanagan River basin, south into the Columbia Plateau and north to the Big Bend of the Columbia River. Many tribes travelled along well-worn trails and river paths each spring and early summer to join in the

---

[5] Chance.

[6] In 1975, Randy Bouchard and Dorothy Kennedy interviewed Martin Louie, a Skoyelpi/Sinixt man who had grown up around the great fishery at the falls. Louie's list of fish included lamprey, sturgeon, salmon, whitefish, carp, peamouth, northern pikeminnow, dace, shiner, sucker, ling cod, sculpin and cutthroat, steelhead, rainbow and bull trout. (Bouchard and Kennedy, "Utilization of Fish.")

[7] In 1810, a North West Company fur trader named Jacques (Jaco) Finlay established Spokane House at the mouth of the river. The first trade fort established in the upper Columbia region, Kootenae House, was built by North West Company trader and surveyor David Thompson in 1808 near Windermere, BC.

[8] Brogan.

harvest. When it came to salmon, there was no boundary. A central cultural law in place assured all who came to the fishery equal access to the abundance. The Salmon Chief oversaw this food distribution. No one left hungry.

***

Marked as "Old Oregon" or "The Columbia District" on early maps drawn by European explorers, the entire Columbia River watershed from source to sea remained borderless and open to free access by many tribes and fur traders in the early 19th century, as it engaged in what would soon be the rapid transformation from an indigenous to a colonial world. Sounding Waters became known as Kettle Falls. Trade forts popped up in several other locations. Still, the tribal nations who had lived along the Columbia and its tributaries for thousands of years were treated largely as political equals by the fur trade.[9] The watershed remained under a loose joint

---

[9] When the Hudson's Bay Company moved its trade fort to Sounding Waters, HBC governor George Simpson and the Salmon Chief Kee-Kee-Tum-Nous agreed that if the tribes supported the HBC's exclusive right to trade in the region, the HBC would leave the fishery entirely to the indigenous people. Simpson observed at the time that the traders would be "able to get food out of stones and sand, and could manage to live very well without fish." The tribes not only controlled the fishery; they could prohibit the HBC from fishing in the river. When Governor Simpson returned to Kettle Falls in 1841 on a stop during his trip around the world, the Salmon Chief called on him again. Simpson was impressed by the chief's word-for-word recitation of the terms of the 20-year-old contract. After Simpson gifted the chief with a capote, a shirt, a knife and a small stock of ammunition, he described how "the old fellow, whose whole wardrobe was the hide of a buffalo, was sent away as happy as a king." (Brogan; Simpson.)

jurisdiction of Britain and the upstart United States of America, both of whom recognized a colonial stake in the region from the river's headwaters to its mouth. The Columbia District was a wild place, rich in resources and open space, one that had not been fenced, segmented or significantly disturbed from its indigenous rhythms.

The tribes and even most of the European fur traders living in the region between 1811 and 1840 had little or no idea that Britain and the United States were, in faraway government headquarters, negotiating to create political boundaries that would permanently alter their livelihoods and systems of government. The diplomatic discussions between these countries, conducted by leaders who never set foot in the region, would have far-reaching consequences. The negotiations are as important for what they *almost* accomplished as for what they did accomplish.

Following the War of 1812, the US and Britain had agreed on the 49th parallel as the dividing line from Manitoba/Minnesota as far west as the eastern slope of the Rocky Mountains. By the mid-1840s, when formal diplomatic discussions began about how to draw the rest of the boundary, the US was strongly asserting its interest in the mouth of the Columbia River as a western seaport. American Protestant missionaries had established settlements in several places between the Willamette Valley in present-day Oregon and the bustling fur trade at Fort Colvile, located beside the Sounding Waters fishery. Britain wished to keep the Columbia District whole and in its possession, as it had been during the fur trade. To this end, it proposed two alternatives. The first boundary would take the path of the Kootenay River down the west slope of the Rockies until it reached the Columbia, and then follow the Columbia River to the sea. The second would follow the height of the Rockies south to the Snake River, then follow the Snake to the Columbia and the Columbia to the sea. In both cases, the countries would share the western seaport. In both cases, present-day Oregon and Washington would be part of Canada, with the Columbia River forming the southernmost geographic boundary between the two countries.[10]

In 1844, US presidential candidate James K. Polk advocated for a border at 54 degrees 40 minutes, which would give over much of present-day British Columbia to the Americans. The rallying cry of Polk's supporters, "fifty-four-forty or fight," contributed to his successful election. Britain's foreign secretary, Lord Aberdeen, was unwilling to push back very hard against the newly elected US government, especially in light of American victories in the War of 1812. Aberdeen proposed a compromise: the 49th parallel extending to the west coast, with the exception of Vancouver Island, which would remain entirely in Britain's control. The US accepted, and on June 15, 1846, the two countries signed the Oregon Treaty (Treaty of Washington).[11]

The boundary between the two countries sliced through hundreds of waterways. Most significantly for the story of the salmon, the Columbia was among them. As agricultural settlement of the

---

[10] The explorer and cartographer David Thompson, the first European to arrive in the upper Columbia region, in 1807, was a strong advocate for the border to be at 45 degrees. He wrote to the governor of the colony of Canada in 1843, painting a clear picture of what Britain stood to lose if the 49th parallel extended all the way to the Pacific Ocean. He described "myriads of fine Salmon … weighing from five to fifty-five pounds," lush vegetation and thick forests. "Whoever settles in this fine country and climate has no wish to leave it." (Jenish.)

[11] Wikipedia, "boundary dispute."

west intensified in the latter half of the 19th century, disputes over water use between the two countries increased. When diplomatic difficulties between the British Dominion of Canada and the US arose over the St. Mary and Milk rivers, the Canadian government approached its southern neighbour with a request to form a "commission or otherwise" to regulate the use of trans-boundary water systems from sea to sea. Negotiations between the two countries resulted in the signing of the Boundary Waters Treaty in 1909. As perhaps its most important legacy, this treaty authorized the formation of an International Joint Commission (IJC) on river management. The commission would have three Canadian and three American representatives. It would possess broad powers to resolve disputes over boundary water that might arise in the future.[12]

The Boundary Water Treaty accepted that a river beginning in Canada could be diverted or managed entirely by Canadians for Canadian interest. When it crossed the border, the waterway became an American river, subject to American ideas for its use. Conversely, a waterway that began in the United States could be under that country's control until it flowed into Canada. According to the new treaty, industrial or agricultural activities that might impact a waterway elsewhere in the system would politely consider the watershed's upstream or downstream national neighbor. This treaty framed water as a navigational, industrial or agricultural tool to serve economic interests, not as a habitat for fish.

It was an important moment in the river's history.

---

[12] International Joint Commission. http://www.ijc.org.

* * *

I wake with my head crammed in under the steering wheel and my feet hanging out the open window. I sit up, listening to the hot wind pulling at the pines. In 1942, prior to the flooding of the river valley behind the Grand Coulee Dam, the US government funded one hurried archaeological survey of the Columbia up to the boundary. The treasures this survey unearthed along 150 miles of river shoreline speak to the wide network of trade and the rich human culture of the pre-colonized upper Columbia landscape. Archaeologists catalogued a whale bone club from the Pacific coast, a polished spoon made from a mountain sheep's horn, abalone disks, a ring formed from a slice of a mountain goat's horn, dice made from beaver teeth, bone needles, wedges and combs.[13] One especially unique item surfaced in the dig: a turquoise pendant, half an inch long, symmetrical and highly polished. It was as if the precious stone had been worn smooth by water itself. Its arrival in the upper Columbia from the distant southwest testifies to the magnetic appeal of the great salmon falls and their abundant harvest.

I pull back onto the road and follow Lake Roosevelt reservoir south as far as Kettle Falls, where I pull off again. The rock shelves that slowed the progress of salmon and held basket traps are now submerged. Only in the rare years when Grand Coulee Dam operators drop the reservoir levels for generator maintenance are any signs of the former falls revealed. The expansive sea of water that covers the falls speaks mostly of absence. There is no sound, no variety and no visible vitality. The singular scent of ponderosa pine instead hovers in the hot, resinous air.

---

[13] Collier, Hudson and Ford.

After only a few hours on the road, I have drifted south into a different place, descending from the wet, cool mountains where I live to find an arid ponderosa pine woodland and rocky bluffs. I stare at the cool water, charged heavily with the spring snowmelt from the north. The water feels empty, lifeless and flat.

Grand Coulee Dam was authorized by the US Bureau of Reclamation during the Depression era. The 1942 completion of the dam predated the CRT and its own dams by at least two decades. In 2014, the BC government drew a firm boundary around impacts from this dam. The loss of the salmon to the upper Columbia region, together with any plans for reintroduction, would not be

The Kettle Falls fishery prior to completion of Grand Coulee Dam. COURTESY OF THE COLVILLE CONFEDERATED TRIBES.

taken into account as part of any CRT renegotiation process.[14] Their rationale for this exclusion was that the salmon and steelhead had already been extirpated by the time the CRT was signed. A response by some policy experts has since suggested the extirpation of the salmon is very much linked directly to the CRT, with the lack of fish passage for ocean salmon at Grand Coulee Dam setting a precedent for future dams upstream. From a look at the history and context of the Grand Coulee project, there seems to be little question that its completion, together with the earlier formation of the political boundary, were the two most significant government policy decisions affecting the formation of the Columbia River Treaty.

***

First and foremost, the Grand Coulee Dam was about moving water around for agriculture.

American farmers flocked to the arid plateau of the Columbia River watershed in the late 19th century, arriving in the middle of some very wet years. When the weather cycle returned to its typical arid pattern, these farmers struggled with the reality that the one million acres of fertile desert spreading around them needed about four times the region's average annual rainfall[15] to be viable farmland. In 1902, the American federal government established the Bureau of Reclamation in order to boost agricultural development in the arid west through storage and canal systems that could "reclaim" water for farming. The bureau's engineering eye settled on

---

[14] BC decision found at http://blog.gov.bc.ca/columbiarivertreaty/ files/2012/03/BC_Decision_on_Columbia_River_Treaty.pdf, accessed December 2014.

[15] 102 centimetres (40 inches) rather than 25 (10 inches).

the plateau just two years later. Everyone could see that the Columbia River was transporting abundant water through the arid desert region, and doing so in a channel well below the level of potential growing areas. How could that water be diverted to where agriculture needed it?

The first serious proposal to construct a reclamation dam followed a 1917 meeting at the office of William M. Clapp, an attorney in tiny Ephrata, Washington. Those attending the meeting had been discussing the theories of the geological formation recently put forward by a geologist named Henry Landes.[16] According to Landes, millions of years earlier, lava had bubbled up from hot fissures in the Earth and oozed across the plateau in molten floods that eventually lay as thick as 1200 metres (4,000 feet). The lava cooled into multiple layers of basalt. Eventually, the Columbia was forced into a path between a lobe of ancient granite and a bulging plain of lava. When glaciers encroached from the north, ice seized hold of the Columbia and its tributaries, creating new barriers. Water flowed and froze in repeated cycles until a large dam of ice blocked the Columbia's flow west across the plateau. Forced to find a new route, the river turned sharply south. Ice continued to block the flow of water coming in from the east. A large inland sea formed behind it, gradually becoming known as Glacial Lake Missoula – 2000 cubic kilometres (500 cubic miles) of water spreading east almost 500 kilometres (300 miles). Over thousands of years, water pressure built up behind this glacial dam until the 760-metre-high (2,500-foot) wall of ice finally gave way. Water gushed southwest across the Interior Plateau. The force of the flood formed three great, temporary

---

[16] Galm.

rivers, flowing like several tidal waves combined. Entire cliffs of basalt broke loose as the river carved a new southwestern path. As it did, masses of glacial silt rippled with it across the plateau.

After hundreds of these repeated floods, the climate warmed and ice gave way. The Columbia River returned to its earlier path through the old channel, at a lower elevation than the one more recently carved by the glacial floods. The channel formed by the flood, known by 1917 as the Grand Coulee,[17] was no longer a water channel but a ravine hosting a dry river of sage, bunchgrass and bitterroot.

Legend has it that at some point in the discussion, Mr. Clapp speculated that if nature could create a flood, why not man? The Grand Coulee *had originally been formed by water,* hadn't it? Clapp didn't see why, with a little ingenuity, the channel now high and dry above the river couldn't host water again. He proposed a dam on the main stem of the Columbia River just at the point where the Grand Coulee intersected with the river. Generators could power pumps to transport the water up from the river channel into the ancient coulee. Once the water reached the coulee, a system of gravity canals could move it south and west, moistening the powdery, rich glacial silt around the struggling agricultural communities of Ephrata, Moses Lake, Stratford and Warden.

The capital of the bone-dry landscape where the idea was born was Ephrata, a place name rooted deep in Western culture. Ephrata derives from the Hebrew word for "fruitful." In the Bible, it refers to the metaphoric and literal transformation of deserts into agricultural landscapes. As if divinely supported, the irrigation idea born in Ephrata withstood competition from another water management

---

[17] From French: *coulée* (lava) flow.

scheme backed by the City of Spokane – to funnel water from Idaho's upper Pend-d'Oreille River across eastern Washington to the good soil by way of canals. After fierce local debate, several studies by engineers and concerted national political effort, the dam at the head of the Grand Coulee finally received formal backing in 1931 from the Bureau of Reclamation. In 1933, the State of Washington set aside $377,000 to begin engineering work.[18]

Pamphlets produced by the bureau during the dam's construction capture the excitement and energy that accompanied the reclamation project. "For sale at dry land prices, ample water from the Columbia River back of Grand Coulee Dam can eventually make a million acres blossom like a proverbial rose."[19] The dam was dubbed the Eighth Wonder of the World, trumping the Egyptian pyramids and even the natural wonder of Niagara Falls. On the inside back cover, a photo of the arid Columbia basin sits beside one of a lush garden, with the caption: "Desolation and reclamation." A 1930 brochure produced by the Columbia Basin Irrigation League in Spokane quoted Dr. Elwood Mead, commissioner of reclamation: "We've got to save these towns, these homes and these people. Banks may break, stocks become worthless, jobs be impossible to secure – but a few acres in the Columbia Basin purchased now will always be a home – and when the great dam is finished a comfortable living for years and years." Alongside this optimism came land speculation, with promises that land purchased at $15 to $20 per acre before the project could be sold at its completion at $100 to $500 per acre.

---

[18] Wikipedia, "Grand Coulee Dam."

[19] Publication of the Great Northern Railway, circa 1933.

The initial design of a 168-metre-high (550-foot) Grand Coulee Dam that could store and pump water up into the desert was reduced due to the economic struggles of the Great Depression to 90 metres (290 feet). This height would generate some electricity but not hold back enough water to support the entire irrigation project. President Franklin Delano Roosevelt visited the site in August 1934, was impressed and endorsed the higher dam. Soon after, congress funded a giant employment project under the Depression-era Public Works Administration. Support from the federal government firmly cemented the twin purposes of the facility: water storage for irrigation and hydro-electric generation.[20]

＊＊＊

I turn off the main highway on the east side of the Columbia to cross Lake Roosevelt reservoir on a ferry to Inchelium. Inchelium is today one of the main communities on the Colville Indian Reservation. In traditional times, it was a village inhabited by the Skoyelpi, one of the 12 tribes on the reservation. Today, many descendants of the upper Columbia's Arrow Lakes Indians, declared "extinct" in Canada by the federal government in 1956, also live here alongside the Skoyelpi.

I pull onto the ferry and park behind a white pickup. When I step out to ask the driver if there is a store on the reservation where I can buy some water, he smiles softly out the car window.

You bet.

I babble for several minutes. He gets out of his truck to light a cigarette. He is slightly built, brown-skinned and has warm, dark eyes.

---

[20] Wikipedia, "Grand Coulee Dam."

When I ask if he is an Arrow Lakes Indian, his crinkly brown face cracks into a smile.

Yeah. I'm Lakes.

I introduce myself and explain that I have written a book about the Arrow Lakes people. He nods and puts out his hand.

I'm Corby Swan.

I explain that I am headed to Grand Coulee Dam and wonder if I can cross the reservation to get there, hoping there will be someplace to camp. I ask more questions, about how long he thinks the shortcut might take and what the road is like. He stamps out his cigarette with a bemused look on his face.

I'll lead you to the store, then on to Twin Lakes. You just follow the road right through the rez. You can camp anywhere on the rez, I guess. So long as it's not somebody's place already.

Later, he waits patiently until I emerge from the store with a jug of water. As he leads me back to the main road, I watch his profile through the rear window, realizing that he has quietly rerouted himself to give me a hand. Has it always been this way? The incessant talking and questions of the arriving culture, the patient if bemused listening by the indigenous people. The displaced ones displacing the ones who call a place home. The indigenous people are doing a lot of listening, though I'm wondering if now, with the treaty, they should be doing more of the talking. They seem to be the ones who know where they are.

I follow Corby's pickup as we climb gently up and away from the reservoir and the hot, arid land around it. We arrive at Twin Lakes, where many descendants of the displaced Arrow Lakes people also live. Fir, cedar and even some hemlock gather around the two natural lakes, tugging my senses momentarily back to the rainforest I have come from. They must feel at home here. With the truck windows all the way down, I breathe in the cool, forested air of late afternoon and continue the climb west, up into the Kettle River Range, waving to Corby as I carry on past.

***

As funding for the construction of the high dam was secured in 1934, the Bureau of Reclamation briefly discussed the possibility of a fish ladder for the salmon swimming up the Columbia to spawn in the Sanpoil, Spokane, Pend-d'Oreille, lower Kootenay, Slocan, Incomappleux and Illecillewaet rivers, among other tributaries of the upper Columbia system. In order to compensate for the added height of the dam, engineers calculated that a fish ladder around the dam would need to be 12 kilometres (7.5 miles) long. Though they determined that it was technically possible to create fish passage, the effort was considered "pointless because there was no way to pass smolts downstream." Others involved in the project suggested that a ladder of this length proceeding upstream would fatigue the fish. It would be costly, as well.[21]

The Canadian response offered no further support for the fish. In 1934, W.A. Found of Canada's Department of Fisheries wrote to the US under-secretary of state, O.D. Skelton, explaining that since the salmon spawning above Grand Coulee Dam in Canada were not part of a *commercial* fishery, Canada had no official interest in preserving the stocks.[22] This lack of interest cleared the way to

---

[21] White.

[22] W.A. Found to O.D. Skelton, October 27, 1934: copy provided by John Harrison, information officer, Northwest Power and Conservation Council, Portland, Oregon.

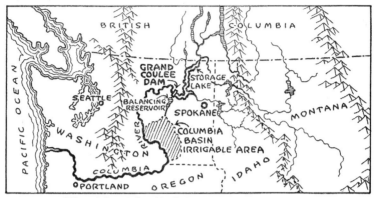

The mighty Columbia drains an immense watershed.

From an American pamphlet "The Columbia Basin Grand Coulee Project,"
1937. Note that while the Arrow and Kootenay Lake regions above the
border are correctly marked on this map, the BC–Alberta border is missing.
TOUCHSTONES NELSON MUSEUM OF ART AND HISTORY.

continue construction of Grand Coulee Dam without considering
fish ladders. Fewer and fewer salmon found their way through the
cofferdams that managed the Columbia's flow during construction.
By August 1938, three shifts of men per day were pouring concrete.[23]
By autumn of that same year, US federal and state fisheries bureaus
were reporting that "no fish will pass the dam next year, or in the
years to come." There was a stated silver lining to the loss. "The end
of the salmon run means construction ... will progress at a much
faster pace."[24]

---

[23] Darland.

[24] Spokane *Spokesman-Review*, November 1, 1938.

***

Corby Swan's suggestion that I shortcut across the reservation turns out to be a fine one. The Gold Mountain Ridge – steep, rocky, and nearly uninhabited by people – is a transportation corridor for large mammals between the Cascades and the Rockies. This is a wildly beautiful and isolated pine forest. By the time I drop down out of the mountains to connect with the Sanpoil River, it feels as if I have driven far enough to get to Grand Coulee Dam, though a quick check of my map tells me I am not quite halfway there. I cruise past lush swaths of red osier and willow, gathered in a verdant curtain along the active upper Sanpoil River's flood plain. The afternoon sun falls further in the sky. Gradually, I notice that the Sanpoil is no longer acting like a river. It has become a reservoir. This "Sanpoil Arm" of Lake Roosevelt reservoir, once densely settled by the Sanpoil tribe, or *snpgwilxex* people, was a desirable location for salmon fishing, with a large weir built across the river every year.[25]

Before its water greets the dammed Columbia, I turn away from today's Sanpoil Arm and head directly west along Manilla Creek Road. Ahead of me, I see the bright orange signs of road work. Gearing down, I ease the pickup to a stop in the shade and settle in for a wait.

***

By 1940, Coulee Dam was the largest concrete structure on the continent, rising 116 metres (380 feet) above the riverbed, spreading a kilometre and a half (nearly a mile) wide and 152 metres (500 feet) thick at its base. As it rose toward its full height of 168 metres

---

[25] Bouchard and Kennedy, *Lake Roosevelt.*

(550 feet), it had quickly become a symbol of survival and future prosperity that entirely eclipsed salmon. That year, the Bonneville Power Administration hired the popular folksinger and composer Woody Guthrie to compose and perform music for a documentary about the brand new dam on the verge of completion. Guthrie spent a month travelling the region, taking in the magnitude of the project and the river it sought to tame. While the documentary never materialized, he did write a number of songs about the river and its new dam:

> Well, the world has seven wonders that the trav'lers always tell,
> Some gardens and some towers, I guess you know them well,
> But now the greatest wonder is in Uncle Sam's fair land,
> It's the big Columbia River and the big Grand Coulee Dam.

The reedy tunes and folksy, rhyming lyrics give voice to the struggles of the settlers all around him: those who had come to the desert in droves during the first decades of the 20th century, intent on farming the arid landscape of the central basin, and those whom the Great Depression had put out of work. "Uncle Sam took up the challenge in the year of thirty-three," Guthrie warbled, "For the farmer and the factory and all of you and me." In the 1930s, Guthrie himself had ridden a wave of refugees, the "Okies" from the catastrophic dust storm period who migrated west along the famed Route 66. With a natural eye for beauty and grandeur, and a commoner's hope for a better world for working-class men, his songs are charged with the hope that human ingenuity would marshal its forces to outwit the climate and conquer the dustbowl. The river – a body of water that Guthrie depicts as munificent as well as magnificent – just might fix all that ailed the country, with a little help from Uncle Sam.

As the project neared completion, the needs of impending war began to diminish somewhat the original purpose of Grand Coulee Dam: to make the desert blossom with irrigation like a biblical Ephrata. The completion of the pumping plant was postponed as focus shifted to the installation of generators to make power, a few of which had been bound for the Shasta Dam project in California but would be put into service first at Grand Coulee until Shasta could be completed. Guthrie captures the project's new purpose:

> Now in Washington and Oregon you can hear the factories hum,
> Making chrome and making manganese and light aluminum.
> And there roars the flying fortress now to fight for Uncle Sam,
> Spawned upon the King Columbia by the big Grand Coulee Dam.

Ironically enough, patriotism also overwhelmed any concerns about the 11 human communities slated to be flooded between the dam and the international boundary, many of them agricultural: Keller, Peach, Lincoln, Gerome, Inchelium, Gifford, Daisy, Harvy, Kettle Falls, Marcus and Boyds. All told, 3,000 people would be displaced. The long-awaited construction of the pumping plant finally began the year after the war. In 1949, A Bureau of Reclamation official articulated the radical shift in cultural attitudes toward water that had been brought on by Depression, drought and then war: "It will be a rare drop of water that goes unused."[26] By 1952, the first irrigation water from the Grand Coulee project had arrived in the arid Columbia basin. It was time to bring the desert to life.

---

[26] Morgan.

***

When I arrive at Grand Coulee Dam, there is no time to take much notice. I need a place to camp before dark. I drive quickly through Electric City and head toward Steamboat Rock State Park. Heading southwest on Route 155 along Banks Lake, I can see how the vast storage reservoir positioned just above the dam takes advantage of the ancient coulee. In the light of a setting sun, the coulee's structured basalt columns rise up from the water's surface like gleaming castles. I turn off at a sign for the state park and drive toward the imposing hunk of basalt that gives it its name. The rock is indeed shaped remarkably like a steamboat. Indigenous stories describe how Coyote once sprinkled some of each of the edible food plants on its surface, as a reminder of his generosity.

I survey the empty, nearly treeless campground filled with asphalt pads for RVs. It's mid-week and there isn't a soul around. The sprinkler system is on, watering the clipped grass. Corby Swan's words come back. *I can camp anywhere on the Rez so long as it's not someone's place already.* I reverse back the way I have come as the sun drops behind the basalt cliffs. Gearing the truck down, I climb up the road that crosses the boundary onto the Colville Reservation. I am headed back toward the Kettle River Range, through rolling sagebrush and a few scattered pines, retracing my path, feeling more at home now. Near the watershed divide for Manilla Creek, faint tire tracks carve a path through the rolling sea of sage and rabbit bush. I turn off impulsively, my tires crushing desert wildflowers that don't appear to have been flattened yet this year. The road ends in a wide hollow, carpeted with vivid yellow balsam-root sunflowers, white desert phlox and soft purple tufts of Douglas's brodiaea.

A few jack pines rise up at the edge of a bluff. Protected by the soft beauty of this place, I unload the truck.

Thank you, Corby, I mutter to myself as I pitch my tent in the falling light.

A dry desert wind blows most of the night, sweeping my mind clean. I dream of seeds laid carefully into soil, then dug up again by an animal's instinctual paws. At dawn, the call of a mourning dove joins other birds fluttering and singing in the flowers around my tent. I drift back to sleep. What does a fish do if it cannot release its own seeds into the natal stream where it wants to die?

When I wake later, the tent is hot and stuffy. I brew a cup of coffee and sit on a chunk of ancient lava, squinting at the mid-morning sun and listening to the jack pines whisper their lonely song. Below the windswept bluff, the land drops into rocky, dry folds. At the base of the bluff, the waters of Lake Roosevelt begin the collection and storage of the river's wild impulses. I try to imagine the carefully managed system being broken apart, the river moving unpredictably again. Salmon carried ocean nutrients through this desert to the moist forests of the uppermost Columbia basin, penetrating the vast upper watershed as only Coyote could,[27] pushing far into the lush folds to deposit the spawn. Salmon was the spine of the people's diet, the bedrock of their relationship with this place.

---

[27] A widespread Salish story describes in various versions how Coyote released the salmon from traps built by sisters near the mouth of the Columbia.

***

Increasing the height of the Coulee dam from 90 to 168 metres (290 to 550 feet) resulted in water from Lake Roosevelt backing up as far as the boundary. The International Joint Commission set up hearings to discuss the impacts of the reservoir, even though, according to the United States, "the necessity for securing the approval of the Commission of the construction and operation of the project might reasonably be questioned." Three brief meetings took place in 1941, in Spokane, Washington, and Trail, BC, immediately prior to the project's completion. At this late date, the meetings were largely a formality. Fish came up once. At the second meeting, in Trail on September 3, in an impromptu statement, W.J.E. Biker, a resident of Nelson, BC, expressed concerned about the dam's upstream impact on fish populations.

Listening was F.A. Banks, the supervising engineer for the Grand Coulee project. Biker said: "We have some of the finest fishing facilities in the world right here in British Columbia, and I should be sorry if by virtue of this dam being constructed the possibility of catching fish in future years should decline, and that is why I am on my feet today to try to tell you that the matter is one which is of importance to us."

Banks responded with plans for a $125,000 fish hatchery to be constructed on a tributary of the Spokane River, nearly 160 kilometres (100 miles) downstream, "for the sole purpose of propagating rainbow trout for stocking the reservoir above the dam. That is purely a game fish proposition; it is the one that Senator Stanley referred to. We are taking care of the game fishermen. We all like to fish down in our country as well as you folks do up here."

Mr. Biker was not about to let the matter rest. At the third hearing in Trail the next day, fish come up again when L.J. Burpee, IJC secretary, read a letter into the record:

September 4, 1941

To the International Joint Commission on Boundary Waters
L.J. Burpee Esq., Secretary
Davenport Hotel,
Spokane, Washington, U.S.A.

RE: Coulee Dam

Gentlemen:
The undersigned have learned with interest of the presentation made by a member of this Board, Mr. W.J.E. Biker, appearing as a private citizen, at your public meeting in Trail yesterday, regarding the effect the Coulee Dam may have on our migratory fish resources in British Columbia and now wish to present to you for your consideration at your hearing in Spokane on Saturday, September 6th the resolution appended hereto.

We desire to state that we are not fully informed as to the habits and behaviour of our migratory fish and are not aware that the Commission has made any investigation to this end.

The appended resolution, which has been prepared by a special committee appointed for the purpose by regular meeting of our Board held to-day, is also supported by the West Kootenay Association of Rod & Gun clubs, in which clubs are incorporated members from the whole district affected.

RESOLUTION:
"RESOLVED that we respectfully ask the International Joint Commission on Boundary Waters to have investigations made by competent authorities in order that the Commission may write

into its Order of Approval sufficient safeguards to protect the interest of British Columbia in this respect."

Respectfully submitted
Nelson Board of Trade
W.G.C. Lanskail, Secretary

In the discussion that followed, F.A. Banks explained that due to the long migration of the salmon by the time they arrive at Grand Coulee, the journey up a fish ladder "would be too great for the fish to undertake." He went on to say that the Bureau of Reclamation had decided to address "the problem of changing the homing instinct of the salmon – to re-educate them to [go] up these smaller streams in place of coming up the Columbia River." When IJC chair A.O. Stanley questioned whether or not fish spawned in a hatchery environment would in fact have any ability to find one of these particular streams, Banks replied that the biologists working on the project "are quite certain" that the homing instinct of a salmon "develops in the fish after it is hatched."

At this point, the discussion ended abruptly and the IJC turned to other matters.[28]

***

Later that morning, when I arrive at the Bureau of Reclamation interpretive centre, the woman behind the counter states her views clearly.

The dam wasn't that big a deal for the salmon. They were just about finished.

---

[28] More discussion of the International Joint Commission hearings on Grand Coulee Dam can be found at http://www.nwcouncil.org/history/InternationalJointCommission.

Out the window opposite the information counter, Grand Coulee's concrete apron provides a fitting backdrop for her firm opinions. As much as I try to accept the modernity and wonder of all the affordable electricity, another thought pushes its way in. Our culture's rush to master one dimension of the river's power has effectively sacrificed another rich, renewable resource. A man behind the counter chimes in, making reference to a visitor who had stopped into the centre last week and complained about how the dams destroyed the ocean salmon runs.

Doesn't he know that the Snake River canals owe their existence to the dams? How can we get these darned environmentalists to see that if we lose those barges, there aren't enough trucks in North America to haul all the wheat out of there?

I have read about the history of barges on the Snake River navigation system, made possible by several large dams built in the 1970s.[29] Much of the wheat going downstream to the Pacific on these barges

---

[29] Wikipedia, "Snake River." The Snake River is the largest of Columbia River tributaries, with its approximately 1600 kilometres (1,000 miles) spreading across six US states. The Rivers and Harbors Act of 1945 authorized the US Army Corps of Engineers to create the Lower Snake River Project and construct several dams to form a navigation channel. Since the early 1990s, there has been ongoing litigation over the impact of these dams on salmon and steelhead migration. One court-ordered program requires release of water through dams to assist salmon. More legal decisions enforcing further protection of salmon have been subject to multiple appeals, undertaken by the federal agencies that operate the dams. In June 2011, Washington congressman Jim McDermott introduced Bill HR2111 laying out a plan to study dam removal. This bill died in committee. For more on Columbia/Snake salmon and the US Endangered Species Act, see http://www.nwcouncil.org/history/EndangeredSpeciesAct.

had been transported by train to the head of the Snake's barge system, from as far away as South Dakota. Railways once did all the work. The man speaks again.

I always say to people: what do you want, fish or bread?

I step quietly away. Could the Columbia basin have bread *and* fish? The human power to rationalize any decision we make includes the wrong ones, of course. The firmer the rationalization, the less possibility for change.

***

In January 1939, the US secretary of the interior, Harold L. Ickes, announced a plan to relocate the dwindling stocks of spawning salmon expected to arrive from the ocean. The US government purchased eight specially equipped tank trucks for the bureau, to capture the fish before they reached the dam. "The 1939 run of Steelheads and salmon will be handled on a temporary but adequate basis," said John C. Page, commissioner of reclamation. The plan, designed by R.D. Calkins, W.F. Durand and W.H. Rich of Stanford University, involved taking the fish destined to spawn above the dam, and planting them in rivers below the dam – the Wenatchee, Entiat, Methow and Okanagan– to enhance fish stocks in these four tributaries. The theory was that the migrating fish would quickly adopt these streams as their new homes and enhance declining runs in those locations in a win-win situation. The federal government would create four hatcheries – three downstream of the dam to produce salmon, and one more above the dam to stock the new 243-kilometre (151-mile) Grand Coulee reservoir with sport fish such as trout. The fish hatchery for the reservoir – funded as a part of the Grand Coulee project – did not last long. The reclamation plan for the ocean salmon and steelhead trout also failed. Predicated on an engineered structure of planting, harvest and intensive management, based on scientific theory, the plan to "re-educate" the salmon had failed. As little as seven years later, substantial mortality of adult salmon was observed both in the hatchery holding ponds and in the more extensive natural holding areas.

The hatcheries were plagued with many problems. Brood stock died, disease was rampant, fish food was considered costly and nutritionally inadequate, the rearing system was not receiving enough water flow, nor, ultimately, was funding meeting the needs of the program. The transplants failed to become established in their new streams as they searched in vain for olfactory clues, for memories of a stone or a current, for any sort of trigger that told them they had arrived home. Today, the large species of chinook that the Salmon Chief had once beckoned into his trap, fish that weighed between 18 and 45 kilograms (40–100 pounds) are considered by some fish biologists to be extinct as a genetic type.

In the indigenous, pre-Contact world of the Interior Plateau, fish and people once inhabited an intuitive rather than theoretical world. At Kettle Falls, the Salmon Chief listened to various seasonal and other-worldly signs to know when it was time to move to the edge of the river. Then, word came from a runner sent by downstream tribes. *They're coming.*

At that point, the Salmon Chief would position the main J-shaped trap above the section of falls that the people called *nlhelhewikn,* "spearing on back." He kept a silent vigil through the night, calling on the power of his guardian spirit – Salmon, the fish they called Good Swimmer, *en-tee-tee-uh.* At sunrise, the chief chose four young men to help him lower the trap into position. He watched carefully until two large chinook – a male and a female – had fallen back into the trap.[30]

The young men lifted the fish from the basket. A chosen woman eviscerated and carefully poached the fish in the water-worn hollows or "kettles" of stone beside the falls. When it was cooked, this first fish was divided gratefully among all present. At the ceremony's end, the bones were returned to the water as an offering of thanks. Only then could the harvest begin.[31]

The position of Salmon Chief was loosely hereditary, a responsibility usually passed within a family. One of the last hereditary Salmon Chiefs, Kee-Kee-Tum-Nous, died in 1862, a victim of smallpox. From about 1866 on, the prayers of the next Salmon Chief, Kin-Kan-Nowha, seemed powerless against the influence of fish wheels operating on the lower Columbia to feed the voracious appetites of

---

[30] Bouchard and Kennedy, *Fish Utilization of the Okanagan-Colville.*

[31] Chief trader Archibald McDonald (cousin of Angus – see note 4) settled at Kettle Falls with his wife and family in 1835. Appointed in 1833, just before a year's furlough back to Britain, he was given the task of expanding the agricultural production and profits at Fort Colvile. Bound by Governor Simpson's agreement with the Salmon Chief (see note 9), McDonald was not free to develop a salmon processing system as he wished. In a letter to settlers at the mission, McDonald demonstrates a simmering racism fuelled by his frustration. "There is no want of salmon now at the falls," he writes in June 1841, "& had the lazy hounds offered such a blessing been only half so industrious as they ought they might have lain up a good standby before the time they say their creed will allow them to commune. Our Salmon Chief," he continues, "has located himself in the mountains to the north of us, masticating deer's meat to his heart's content, & sends word from time to time to his less fortunate dupes on no account to go near the falls, or trespass on the established law, until it be his will & pleasure to say the *thing is very good.*"

new canning facilities. The number of spawning fish returning to Kettle Falls fell rapidly after that, as the people watched their life-sustaining resource disappear. In 1896, Sipas received the power from Kin-Kan-Nowha. By 1930, a decade before Grand Coulee's completion, Sipas had died, and with him, the title of the Salmon Chief.[32]

James Bernard, then chief of the Arrow Lakes/Sinixt tribe, des-cribed the fishery at that time: "Sometimes we get five or six fish a day in the baskets for all the Indians of all the tribes – one day we got 30 fish – some days we get none. Before the whites destroyed the salmon fishing, 300 to 400 fish a day were caught in the baskets at Kettle Falls, besides the hundreds caught with spears and gaff hooks. Some Indians used to catch 20 to 30 salmon a day by themselves that way. Now a person may fish all day with a spear and never get a fish."[33]

* * *

In 1939, members of many tribes gathered at Kettle Falls from around the Interior Plateau for the "Ceremony of Tears," to say goodbye to the salmon. Some of them comforted themselves with Coyote's prophecy: he had gone away in the West but would be back, and when he came, he would bring back the salmon.

---

[32] *Rawhide Press*. Established in April, 1958, *Rawhide Press* is a monthly community newspaper owned and operated by the Spokane Tribe of Indians in Wellpinit, Washington. The Spokane Tribe archives all copies of the newspaper in its cultural office.

[33] Ibid.

***

I leave the interpretive displays and step into the fierce desert sun. The imposing hydro-electric project has restructured the soft bluffs and dramatic basalt hillsides of the plateau desert. A cleanly drawn geometry now tells water exactly where it can go and what it can do. At the centre of this project is the dam itself – an impressive and effective wall of concrete. A maze of transmission wires loop evenly across the air, supported by a forest of steel towers. Neatly placed rip-rap covers the riverbank below the dam's tailrace. Before the Columbia River Treaty between the US and Canada, water passed over the spillway regularly. Greater efficiencies in the upper system made the spill unnecessary and wasteful, other than for a few days, during high-water spring melt. For a number of years, a light show used to stain the foaming overflow with the story of the dam's construction and accomplishments. The light show has been updated to include some of the immeasurable losses and is now broadcast on a concrete surface that is almost always dry. Thanks in part to storage in the Canadian portion of the system, generators at Grand Coulee process water more efficiently than they ever have.

I return to my makeshift campsite, pack my tent and set out north again across the sagebrush forest. In the 1970s, Sinixt/Skoyelpi elder Martin Louie told researchers about hemp fishing lines and nets, how the women split apart the stems from hemp dogbane (*Apocynum cannabinum*) and rolled the fibres back and forth across their thighs with the palms of their hands. From the rhythm of their own flesh, the women produced a string sturdy enough to capture the river's flesh, the wild and profuse salmon species. Hemp string was long, strong and resilient, in many ways like the flow of the Columbia River system used to be, with its fish, floods and pulsing rhythms.

Settlers brought values from elsewhere, values that were not woven into the landscape. The new people did not realize that the river's great salmon runs in the lower reaches depended upon the rich spawning grounds upstream of Grand Coulee, in the mountains where I live.

In *The Gift*, Lewis Hyde compares the returning salmon to good literature. A spawning fish is like poetry or fine writing, something in possession of "reservoirs of available life." For Hyde, the salmon is a mysterious container sustaining both the human heart and the body's appetites. The traditions of the first salmon dictated that the Salmon Chief must always return the bones to the water, in a gesture of reciprocity practiced also by Coast Salish tribes. Hyde sees this as a formalizing of the give-and-take relationship between human culture and salmon, a reciprocity that acknowledges a "participation in and dependence upon, natural increase." Hyde fears that destroying the natural, renewable wealth of the salmon is to risk consciously destroying ourselves.

Several years ago, the Colville Confederated Tribes in the US and the Okanagan Nation Alliance in Canada launched an ambitious salmon restoration on the Okanagan River, a major tributary that flows out of Canada to join the Columbia downstream of Grand Coulee Dam. Though this tributary connected to the Columbia below Grand Coulee Dam, a variety of other factors had resulted in the salmon runs being reduced to a shadow of their former numbers.[34] Fish biologists gradually transformed the channelized,

---

[34] The lakes in the Okanagan watershed that extend north into Canada once formed about 40 per cent of the watershed's total juvenile rearing habitat for ocean sockeye.

straightened river into one that could twist and turn again, to host spawning eddies. Tribal people gathered for salmon festivals, standing by the water, singing songs and beating drums, calling the spirit of Salmon home. This combination of the rational and the intuitive has created results: 108,000 salmon returned in 2008 and 200,000 in 2010 and 2011. On Tuesday, June 26, 2012, 41,573 sockeye passed through the fish ladders around Bonneville Dam on the lower Columbia *in a single day*, headed upstream. By the time the spawning season was over that year, nearly half a million sockeye had returned to the Okanagan River.

Many scientists, ecologists and technicians say that the return of salmon to the upper reaches of the Columbia watershed above Grand Coulee Dam is a romantic and impossible dream. It would be too expensive. There are too many introduced predators. It couldn't work now that the river is a reservoir. It is an odd and unnatural lake. It's too warm, and it will only get warmer with climate change. It's too still. Salmon need flowing rivers, not stable and predictable reservoirs.

Yet the success of the Okanagan sockeye restoration has provided inspiration. The 15 united American tribes in the Columbia basin show little interest in rational arguments. They have recently produced a statement of values about how the Columbia River can and should be restored under a renegotiated CRT. Salmon are at the top of their list. In general, the tribes want restoration of the ecosystem to guide river operations just as much as hydro-power efficiencies and flood control do. Initial responses by the US review team have been promising enough, with a "third leg" being added to the original river stool of power production and flood control. Now the review team talks regularly, if vaguely, about "ecosystem function" as a guiding principle of a reconfigured Columbia River system. At a symposium on the CRT held in Polson, Montana, in October 2012, tribal leaders pushed their ecosystem demands up a notch. Ecosystem health should not be one of three interests governed by the treaty, they asserted; ecosystem considerations should be the stool itself. One tribal chief told those listening that human beings are not "in charge of the ecosystem" but are part of it. The ecosystem is not a side interest, he said. It is us. Central to the restoration of the ecosystem is allowing the river to flow in support of ocean salmon. The tribes are keen to help the salmon find its way to the upper Columbia spawning grounds: across the boundary, up through the Arrow Lakes, and beyond, threading the shadowed river gorge spanned by Revelstoke Dam, over the top of Mica Dam's high, swollen concrete lip, and on to the headwaters.

One tribal leader at the symposium said that restoration of salmon might not happen in his lifetime, but that this did not dull his desire to work toward such a goal. Indigenous leaders reminded government, corporate and academic interests that salmon cannot see the border between the two countries, nor does skepticism justify turning away from a job that needs to be done. They asserted that if the salmon are invited above Grand Coulee, they would continue north to the cool waters of the upper basin. Telemetry data has already demonstrated that when fish arrive at the reservoirs, they plunge below the warm surface and find the cooler, deeper water to continue upstream. If they could, they would reclaim spawning habitats or find new ones. They would survive.

When I return to Canada, the place where the wet Columbia Mountains give birth to the marvels of the Columbia's powerful flow, I feel that I have been to another world. Between these mountains and the sea sits the dry desert where the historical miracle of salmon passage has revealed its paradoxes. It humbles me to think that the Good Swimmer once linked the mountains where I live with the Pacific Ocean by swimming through the desert.

Can the same fish now span two countries?

***

Grand Coulee Dam was one of several major projects undertaken on the American portion of the Columbia River in the first half of the 20th century. The US government also commissioned Rock Island Dam (completed 1933) and Bonneville Dam (completed 1938). At that point, the development of hydro-electric systems on the Columbia rose up to the boundary but no further. North of the boundary, Duff Pattullo, the Depression-era premier of BC, had briefly initiated interest in development of the Canadian Columbia. When he wrote to the prime minister, Mackenzie King, in 1937 to ask for a study of potential benefits or damage in "thorough development of hydro-power on either side of the line," King's position was to have far-reaching historical consequences. It was perhaps best to delay any study or development of the Columbia River, he said, until the Americans approached Canada.[35]

---

[35] Stanley.

2. Big Water Year

A Salish tribal prayer to the four directions speaks of the north as the place that "changes the world." Looking north up the Columbia, "water gathers all the deteriorated stuff and takes it south, piles it up on each side of the shore, and what goes out on the ocean will never return. And we have a brand new world in spring. The high waters take everything out, wash everything down."[1]

Just across the river from Nelson, BC, sits a pictograph high on a cliff. Though there appears to be no easy access to this cliff, the location has always made sense to me, viewed through the lens of history. Water marks on rock cliffs on Kootenay Lake's West Arm demonstrate how this portion of the lower Kootenay River system once flooded up to 20 feet above today's high water levels. Such could be the impact of a spring flood in the West Arm, before settlers blasted riverbed channels downstream, and before Libby Dam controlled the input of water from upstream. When the water was high in spring, a pictograph artist might more easily float to this cliff-site in a canoe, then use ropes or climbing skills to get the rest of the way.

---

[1] Louie.

Watching the river closely, the indigenous people learned to locate settlements where they knew the water was unlikely to go. In their upper Columbia landscape, it was important to allow the water to cleanse, renew and transform. It transported nutrients and fish fry to new places. It charged the flood plain with fresh minerals. Over several millennia, the upper Columbia's Salish tribes adapted their lifestyles to the water's shifting movements. They grew more and more resilient and intelligent in how they cooperated with a force that they could not alter or control. They built more and more villages above the reaches of the annual flood plain. They learned to ride the charged current of spring snowmelt downstream to the annual salmon fishery at Sounding Waters in June. Often, families would not journey upstream until autumn, when canoes loaded with dried fish for winter could navigate a much quieter river.[2]

The timing of annual spring freshet in the Columbia basin has always been mysterious, attached as it is to the unpredictability of weather. In years of lean winter snowfall followed by an early, warm spring, the mountains empty their light load more quickly. In heavy snowfall years, when cool spring weather delays the annual melt, the water might be forced into a seasonal bottleneck. If such a cycle includes very hot weather and bouts of spring rain, lots of water enters the system from more than one source at the same time. Hydro-electric engineers call the result a "big water year." When it happens, the upper Columbia watershed – defined by narrow valleys, high mountains and steep terrain – fills rapidly to the brim. Water swells up out of its channel and temporarily enters side channels or flood plains. It "takes everything out, washes everything down." Water must find a way.

---

[2] Wynecoop.

***

Three years after the completion of Grand Coulee Dam, the US and Canada made a joint request for the IJC to investigate the feasibility of greater use of the river's resources. The IJC formed the Columbia River Engineering Study Group. This same year, a Canadian company, Cominco, completed the Brilliant Dam at the mouth of the Kootenay River, to serve growing industrial power needs and explore the possibilities of producing heavy water (deuterium oxide) for atomic weapons.[3] This brought to five the number of private dams on the lower Kootenay River system operated by Cominco and its corporate subsidiary, West Kootenay Power and Light: Upper and Lower Bonnington (1897 and 1907), Corra Linn (1932), South Slocan (1928) and Brilliant (1944). Ninety-seven per cent of the hydro-power potential on the lower Kootenay River west of Kootenay Lake had been captured, yet no dams existed on the main stem of the Columbia River, nor were there any survey maps of the upper basin's landscape.

In 1948, the Canadian Department of Mines and Surveys initiated a series of maps, estimated to cost Canada $1-million. The work of the IJC was at this point generally cooperative in spirit. As the painstaking survey of the upper Columbia basin began, the US continued its own independent plan to study the river. In February 1947, it published a study describing the upper Columbia region as a "subdivision" of the larger basin, an abundant source of the Columbia's powerful hydrology. "Water," the report said, "is the foremost natural asset of this subdivision, and the resources of water power, both developed and undeveloped, are large." Specifically, the report

---

[3] Mouat.

recognized "numerous lakes, large and small, possess utility not only for navigation, but also for storage and regulation of flow to produce a more beneficial use of the water supply of the Columbia River Basin. These storage possibilities are of manifest interest to the development of the basin in the United States as, similarly, are favorable storage sites in the United States of interest to Canada."[4]

In the midst of all these careful studies about how to take advantage of the "natural assets" of the upper Columbia basin, the weather threw in a wild card. That spring, snow accumulations were measured at 120 to 142 per cent of normal in the mountains of central and northern Washington and southeastern BC. Cool rain continued well into May, with more snow added in the high elevations.

A big water year had begun.

May 19–22, 1948:
On the Lardeau River north of Kootenay Lake, the rapidly rising water nearly strands a logging crew. Rivers rise rapidly due to warm weather, followed by fresh bouts of heavy rain.[5]

May 24–25:
A tributary of the upper Kootenay River floods, sweeping away a dozen homes in Kimberley, BC, forcing evacuations and washing out the rail line that serves the nearby Sullivan Mine. The Elk River surges toward Fernie, BC, with "unabated fury."[6] *Dikes protecting Creston, BC, farmlands threaten to burst. Flash flooding occurs in Grand Forks, BC. The Kootenay River slices through dikes protecting 40,000 acres of farmland in Bonners Ferry, Idaho.*

---

[4] US Department of the Interior, *The Columbia River.*

[5] *Nelson Daily News*, May 21, 1948.

[6] Ibid., May 24, 1948.

In the late 19th century, waves of arriving settlers had no knowledge of the typical snow-charged rhythms of the upper watershed. They built towns and farms on the inviting flood plains, where the soil was rich and soft and the terrain flat. When the snowmelt and spring rains were heavy, water overflowed the banks as it always had. Now it threatened livelihood, crops and the safety of people who lived on the flood plains.

May 26–28:

Evacuation of Bonners Ferry begins. The West Arm of Kootenay Lake, fed by the same surging Kootenay River, rises one foot every 24 hours.[7] The Canadian Red Cross, Army and Air Force rush tents to 140 families in Kimberley. Farms in Edgewood, BC, are underwater. According to C.E. Webb, chief engineer for the British Columbia Department of Mines and Resources, the Columbia River is rising now at a rate of two feet per day. The warm weather continues, with peak run-off still ten days away. The State of Washington prepares to evacuate 13,000 to 14,000 people from a trailer camp serving the Hanford atomic energy project on the mid-Columbia. The lower reaches of the Columbia River are already eight feet over flood stage. Another surge of melt is headed toward the basin's densely populated Portland, Oregon, metropolitan area.[8]

History records only two major floods on the Columbia prior to 1948: one in 1876 and the other in 1894. In the latter flood, the bustling and recently constructed towns of Cascades, Washington, and Trail, BC, both built close to the river's main channel, were entirely swept away.

---

[7] *Spokane Daily Chronicle,* May 24, 1948.

[8] *Nelson Daily News,* May 27, 1948.

For the next 60 years, no great floods occurred. The Columbia developed a reputation among water engineers as a river with high annual volume, but not necessarily a river subject to catastrophic floods. Despite its status as the fourth-largest watershed for water volume in North America, the Columbia did not and still does not compare to the Mississippi or the Missouri when it comes to floods of great magnitude reaching wide into the flood plain and beyond. In the mid-century US, dams specifically designed to address flood control were given a low priority compared to those that created electricity or transported water to dry agricultural areas.[9]

On May 29, the Snake River, the largest and southernmost tributary of the Columbia in the US, reached the peak discharge of its snowmelt, one week before the upper watershed in Canada reached its peak. The Snake's 1600-kilometre-long (1,000-mile) river sent the discharge south and west toward Portland and Vanport, Oregon. The 1948 flood was about to completely upend cultural attitudes toward the Columbia River.

May 29–30:

Elmer Fisher, forecaster with the Washington State weather bureau, predicts that the cities of Portland and nearby Vanport will be safe from the peak of the Columbia's flood. He predicts high water there on June 1. Built on an active flood plain, Vanport is actually 30 feet below the level of the river. It has, since 1942, provided temporary housing for shipyard workers, many of them African-American. Fisher cautions as he gives his prediction that it is based on incomplete data.

---

[9] The Northwest Power and Conservation Council. http://www.nwcouncil.org.

The crest of snowmelt and rain reaches Vanport on May 30 at 4:05 p.m.; residents there have not been warned to evacuate. The freshet breaches a makeshift railway dike and water pours "through the town like ocean breakers."[10] *Within ten minutes, Vanport begins to dissolve under six feet of water. The prefabricated houses are lifted from their foundations and "ground to pieces."*[11] *Sixteen bodies are recovered and thousands of people are left homeless.*

Snow is a natural reservoir, storing the potential energy of water through the dormant winter season. As the weather warms, the snow releases this energy, beginning on the valley floor and moving up into the higher reaches of the mountains until most of the seasonal accumulation has transformed into moving water on its way to the sea. The snow-charged landscape of the Columbia basin had evolved over tens of thousands of years, as had the aquatic and terrestrial creatures and plants that knew its rhythms well. The freshet carried young fish from spawning streams. It temporarily flooded wetlands and plains, depositing the rich sediments it had picked up and carried down from mountaintops and the sides of steep slopes.

May 31–June 2:
Conconully, in Okanogan County, Washington, floods; 25 per cent of its buildings are damaged or lost, and 2,000 people are homeless. President Harry S. Truman declares the Pacific Northwest a disaster area. The crest of freshet enters the north section of the city of Portland. Spawning salmon are seen swimming across the flooded

---

[10] *Nelson Daily News,* May 30, 1948.

[11] Spokane *Spokesman-Review,* June 2, 1948.

Washington State Route 99 in Cowlitz County. The Willamette River, a tributary of the lower Columbia, tops a Portland seawall. The Columbia is now at flood stage for almost 75 per cent of its main stem. Throughout the upper watershed, roads, rail lines and ferry ramps have flooded, interrupting transportation systems.[12]

June 4–10:

BC's chief engineer, C.E. Webb, flies over the southern part of the province and observes that a significant snowpack still exists over the 1800-metre (6,000-foot) elevation. A heat wave across southern British Columbia and central Washington begins. The Columbia crests a second time, and dikes finally give way at Creston, flooding 7,700 acres of farmland. On June 9, after four days of unseasonably high temperatures, the Columbia is still rising – over a foot every 24 hours, as measured at Revelstoke, BC. The town of Cusick, Washington, floods. Everywhere in the upper watershed, enormous quantities of driftwood and floating debris threaten bridges and interrupt ferry services.

Extreme spring freshets always carry a high concentration of debris. Sediment deposits in especially high flood years are potent with nutrients. The big water scours loose mineral-rich material and sends it toward the oceans, depositing these nutrients in wetlands and riparian systems all along the way. Minute particles of sediment float like tiny birds on currents of watery wind. Young fish enjoy the anonymity and safety from predators that the turbid water offers. Gravel slips and slides easily along stream channels, rubbing itself clean and gathering into the freshly washed beds where fish choose to spawn. Boulders, large trees and rocks

---

[12] *Nelson Daily News,* June 3, 1948.

are rolled, dragged or skipped along by the current. The faster and more powerful the water, the more sediment and gravel is moved, the more the river is affected. When the water recedes, the river channel has been changed. This change provides a variability that gives natural river systems their variety, liveliness and resilience.

June 12:
The river flow measured at Grand Coulee Dam finally peaks at 18,800 cubic metres (637,800 cubic feet) per second, more than three times the annual average.[13]

The 1948 flood was classified as a "100-year flood," one of such severity that is statistically likely to occur only once every 100 years. It could happen more frequently than that but then not repeat again for some time. By the time the water receded, damage to human property was estimated at US$100-million in 1948 currency values. Fifty people died, 120,000 were evacuated and 38,000 lost their homes. When President Truman visited the region, he expressed determination to build the dams and other structures needed to control the nation's rivers. A report published that October by the Army Corps of Engineers unsurprisingly urged lawmakers to fund flood control projects for the Columbia basin, warning that "a recurrence of a flood of 1894 magnitude would cause damage estimated at over $350-million."[14]

The conflict between the natural function of a snow-charged river and more recent patterns of settlement had finally come to a head,

---

[13] *Floods of May–June 1948 in Columbia River Basin,* available at http://pubs.usgs.gov/wsp/1080/report.pdf.
[14] US Army Corps of Engineers, 308 Report HD531, October 1, 1948.

confirming to American engineers and hydro-power executives that if the river basin was to be properly managed exclusively for human interests, Canada would need to pitch in to provide some engineered flood control.

June 15:
Twenty-five days after a logging crew narrowly escaped being stranded by the rising Lardeau River, the Nelson Daily News reports that the rivers in the region have begun to recede.

In the days and weeks following the catastrophic flood, questions arose about why Grand Coulee Dam had not been able to protect downstream communities. Frank A. Banks, chief engineer for the Grand Coulee project, explained that the dam's primary roles were to provide power and storage for irrigation. When a dam is constructed for these purposes, he said, it must be kept relatively full, not emptied in preparation for the influx of spring freshet. He went on to explain that even if Grand Coulee's reservoir had been completely emptied in preparation for the spring freshet, the force and volume of the freshet would have refilled the reservoir in just five days.[15]

Banks's explanation articulates the key reason why Americans viewed trans-boundary flood control of the Columbia to be essential: making full use of Grand Coulee for electrical power generation and irrigation meant sacrificing flexibility to supply flood control during extreme-flow years such as 1948 – and Grand Coulee would not have had enough storage to deal with the high flows that year. The 1948 flood, Banks suggested, had adequately

---

[15] Spokane *Spokesman-Review,* June 6, 1948.

demonstrated that if Americans wanted flood control during extreme events, as well as the ability to produce power and to irrigate when they wanted, they would need international help.

The 1947 study of the Columbia basin's power potential conducted by the US government had already revealed that in American eyes, the Canadian mountain landscape was a geographic setting perfectly suited to storing water. This capacity ran counter to another upper Columbia basin land use supported by Canada's federal public policies in the region: the orchards, farms and ranches established on land released for sale by Canadian Pacific Railway. By the mid-20th century, the narrow valleys of the Columbia and Kootenay rivers had numerous agricultural communities.

The year after the flood, Canada appointed General A.G.L. McNaughton to chair the Canadian section of the IJC. A retired commander of the Canadian Forces in Europe, McNaughton had earned a reputation as a man of character and spirited nationalism when he convinced Churchill and Field Marshal Montgomery that Canadian forces should be allowed to retain their separate identity, rather than be absorbed into the British Army. His combination of patriotism, fair-minded clarity, military experience and strength served him well as he faced off against his American counterpart on the commission: General Istchner, head of the US Army Corps of Engineers.[16]

Many members of the Columbia River Engineering Study Group formed in 1944 had been trained in and influenced by war. They had returned from the battlefield just in time to watch a great flood threaten human personal safety in the Pacific Northwest.

---

[16] J.D. McDonald.

As if implementing the latest battle plan, McNaughton and Istchner mounted an engineering offensive to control and manage the Columbia's extreme flows to smooth it out and make it safe. Only a managed river could create a steady supply of electricity. Only a tightly controlled river could protect the people from what had become a dangerous enemy of urban development and river-bottom agriculture: the Columbia's annual spring floods.

McNaughton's view of the development of the Columbia was predictably sovereign for a career army man. The upper watershed belonged to Canada. Reservoirs and generators located further up the watershed gave Canada more control over its water.

In 1951, to provide flood control and generate power, the US proposed a six-million-acre-foot (MAF) dam at Libby, Montana, with a reservoir backing 67 kilometres (41 miles) into Canada. McNaughton rejected this plan outright. The BC government also weighed in with its displeasure over the idea. McNaughton proposed instead to divert the upper Kootenay River into the Columbia unless the US agreed to share any power benefits from Libby Dam. McNaughton's proposal was possible as a result of the unique topography of the Rocky Mountain Trench, where the Columbia and the Kootenay flowed in opposite directions from their origins, within a mile of each other. The US responded to McNaughton's counter-proposal by claiming that Canada did not have the right to divert Kootenay River water and keep it in Canada for sovereign development of hydro-electric power.[17]

---

[17] Swainson, 56ff. Given the complexity and exhaustive nature of this policy history, all further references to Swainson's work will include page numbers.

A tug-of-war over the proposed Libby Dam had begun. During the next decade, the merits of the project, and the question of how to control the upper Columbia watershed, would be discussed and debated.

***

I hear agencies and governments from both Canada and the US refer often to the flooding of Vanport as an example of the dangers of a river that is allowed to run free. *Look at what could happen again*, the rhetoric goes, *if we loosen the tight hold dams have on the Columbia River system to return to it some of its natural spring freshet.* In fact, Vanport is the poorest of examples, given the complexity of the story behind the simple statistics often referenced in our contemporary debate. Lost in the musty files of history is the lack of a clear evacuation order for that community, even when the risk was identified. Lost is the fact that the city was constructed on a known flood plain. History actually demonstrates that human beings are far more adaptive to natural systems than it sometimes appears. Vanport has become less a historical event than part of a rationale for continuing to operate the Columbia system at status quo.[18] Can we stop seeing the river as a villain and increase our own resilience and adaptability to natural rhythms? Can we learn to co-exist with water that wants to change the world?

---

[18] The Oregon Encyclopedia, "Vanport." http://www.oregonencyclopedia.org/articles/vanport/#.vsjxyzmrkcw.

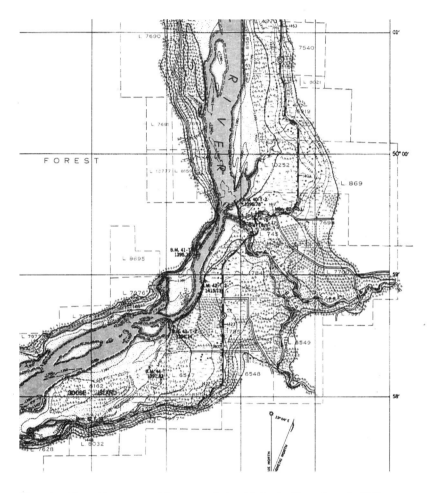

Map sheet from the survey of the upper Columbia basin, Department of Mines and Resources, Surveys and Engineering Branch, 1956.

3. Elections, an Extinction and the Mapping of Graves

In 1952, W.A.C. Bennett was elected premier of BC as leader of the Social Credit party.[1] An entrepreneur and small businessman who came to be known as the "black top premier" for his development of the road system in the province, Bennett was fiscally conservative yet intent on corporate growth and prosperity. Early on, he signalled that he wanted to "modernize" the province and its economy, and do so in a way that would not drain the government's bank accounts. Bennett's ideology, personality and effectiveness as a leader positioned him as a significant player in the negotiation process unspooling from the question of whether or not to approve Libby Dam.[2]

---

[1] The Social Credit party was originally created after the Depression to address monetary reform. By the time Bennett took over as leader in BC, it had developed into a populist conservative party – a natural fit with Bennett's fiscal conservatism. Under his leadership, the "Socreds" experienced seven consecutive victories in two decades, making Bennett the longest-serving premier of BC. For more, see Wikipedia, "W.A.C. Bennett."

[2] Mitchell.

The year after Bennett's election, legal experts confirmed to the IJC that, under the 1909 Boundary Waters Treaty, Canada did have the right to divert the south-flowing Kootenay River into the north-flowing Columbia. With this right affirmed, McNaughton's position on diversion became a real threat to US hopes for a hydro-electric and flood control megaproject at Libby. It also became important leverage in the process of negotiating a solution to the water dynamics and power needs of the entire basin. Without water flowing south from the upper Kootenay, the Libby project did not make sense. McNaughton next suggested that the US could go ahead with Libby Dam if it promised to give Canada 50 per cent of the power produced there.

In 1953, the US withdrew the proposal from the IJC.

Through the leverage of Canada's right to divert, McNaughton presented two clear choices to the US: use Canada's water and share the proceeds, or don't expect to have the water available. Under Canadian law, provinces govern the use and development of natural resources, yet the Columbia's international watershed also made it subject to federal involvement. With the right to divert now assured, the Canadian federal government appeared to be in a position to direct the development of the upper Columbia watershed in its best interest.[3]

As if to trump the federal government's lead on river development, W.A.C. Bennett announced in 1954 a provincial agreement with the American corporation Kaiser Aluminum. Kaiser would construct

---

[3] In order, the three largest tributaries to the Columbia are the Snake (entirely in the US); the Kootenay (flowing through both countries); and the Pend-d'Oreille (also flowing through both countries).

a dam in Canada on the Columbia River, a handful of miles upstream of the international boundary near Castlegar, BC. The estimated C$25-million project would be financed entirely by the company. The hydro-generating dam would flood the main stem of the Columbia River valley upstream for over 170 kilometres (100 miles) to the river's annual average high water mark and store four MAF. The agreement stipulated that Kaiser must return 20 per cent of the power to BC.

Bennett's enthusiastic acceptance of Kaiser's proposal for a "low" dam storing four MAF reflected his practical politics: make industry pay for what industry uses. Develop the provincial economy at the same time. The Canadian federal government did not approve of Bennett's stroke of independence, nor did it like the sound of receiving only 20 per cent of the power benefits, especially in light of McNaughton's recent success in arguing for 50 per cent of Libby's power production.[4]

That same year, the US reapplied to the IJC for permission to build Libby Dam on the Kootenay. IJC chair McNaughton began to talk about potential for a dam near Mica Creek, on the Columbia's Big Bend. In January 1955, the federal government passed the International Rivers Improvement Act (Bill 3), entrenching a requirement for a federal licence for all projects on international rivers[5] and effectively upending Bennett's deal with Kaiser. Bennett grew annoyed by what he saw as federal incursion into provincial economic development. McNaughton's all-Canadian vision continued

---

[4] For more on the role of the Kaiser proposal in feeding division between the federal and provincial governments, see Swainson, 57–65.

[5] Swainson, 115.

to solidify in the meetings with the IJC. His own ideas developed into a plan for a low dam similar to the Kaiser proposal in location and size, and a high dam at Mica, made more productive by plans to divert and dam the upper Kootenay-Columbia system in the Rocky Mountain trench. McNaughton's plans would effectively control the water originating in both rivers and, he believed, seal Canada's water sovereignty.[6]

Formal diplomatic discussions between the US and Canada about the Columbia development began in 1956. The US continued to propose Libby Dam to the IJC. McNaughton continued to resist the proposal. His consistency inspired Montana senator Mike Mansfield to conclude that "General McNaughton is one of the most determined men to come up against in negotiations. He is an extreme nationalist, and I say this in a good sense." McNaughton, for his part, was fond of commenting that the Americans "want us to give them a gold watch for the price of a bit of tinsel." Positioning between the two countries continued.[7]

As the painstaking work of creating survey maps of the upper basin drew to a close that year, the Canadian federal bureaucracy had already completed another process that was to have its own impact. Order in Council no. 1956-3, filed on January 5, 1956, declared the Arrow Lakes Indian Band of the upper Columbia region "extinct." A reserve of 255 acres located at Oatscott on the Columbia River main stem near Burton, BC, reverted to the status of Crown land. To follow the paper trail through historical documents over the 50-odd years of this small reserve's existence is to walk through a

---

[6] Swainson, 62.

[7] Swettenham.

troubled forest of racism and misguided government policy, forces that were able to effectively scrub the Sinixt from the region's historical landscape as plans to flood the heart of their traditional territory continued.

* * *

More than a decade ago, I met a government worker who had just rescued a set of the 1956 maps from the dumpster at the back of an office building. Immediately perceiving their historical value, he made digital copies. When he learned about my interest in the river and its history, he offered me some of my own. One day, two CDs arrived in the mail addressed to me. In the images I found a world of unrecognizable variety and detail, the record of a natural river ecosystem since flooded by three CRT reservoirs.

The surveyors made full use of symbols that meticulously mark marshes, cottonwood forests, orchards, hay meadows, currents shaped by the depth of stream bed, and the sinuous shape of the meandering upper Columbia and Kootenay rivers. Whenever I consult the maps, the details of this landscape put me under a spell, so much so that I can easily forget why I have pulled them out in the first place.

Today, I am looking for the Oatscott Indian Reserve, the only authorized land for the Sinixt in Canada, set aside by the federal government for use between 1902 and 1956.[8] I shuffle through the stack until I find map sheet number 17. What surprises me when I locate the land opposite Burton is its size relative to the 240-kilometre-long (150-mile) Arrow Lakes valley. The reserve is a pin-dot in the expansive river region once navigated by Sinixt canoes. Though I

---

[8] The term "reserve" is used in Canada, "reservation" in the US.

am not sure why I would be surprised. Colonial conquest reduced indigenous lands to a pin-dot over and over again, across the continent. The Sinixt pin-dot phenomenon only hits a little harder because of the extinction.

Visiting Oatscott today is a far more difficult process than finding it on a 1956 survey map. A portion of the reserve delineated on the map is, of course, now underwater. What remains to be seen above the high water mark of the reservoir is a narrow slice of steep shoreline at the base of a high bluff, with rocky forest behind that. To add to its marginal status, the memory of Oatscott is on the road-less west shore of the Arrow reservoir.[9] If I am going to follow the tale of Oatscott to its end, I will need a boat. I want to find the granite slab protecting several graves of Arrow Lakes people who were moved up into the woods after their bodies were exposed by the shifting reservoir silt back in 1977.

My friend Charlie Maxfield has lived in the Arrow Lakes valley all his life. He was 12 years old when the survey maps to assist CRT planning were completed. He was a teenager when the treaty was signed; in his early 20s when the valley was flooded. He watched as the water rose to cover heaving gravel bars where sturgeon had wallowed, his best friend's family farm, then a favourite swimming beach, then wetlands where ducks and other waterfowl bred. Charlie, unlike many displaced residents, did not move away. Over the years, he has bought and sold land, worked as a logger, helped install generators in one of the region's many dams and generally found any way he could to make a living.

As he edged toward retirement, Charlie spent more and more time on the shoreline of the reservoir, walking the silted drawdown

---

[9] A logging road does offer seasonal access.

or putting around in his aluminum boat, the sort known in the region as a "tinner." He became a collector of stone artifacts from the culture of the Arrow Lakes Indian inhabitation, stretching back 5,000 years, which is how I first met him. I've been out with Charlie a few times – in his boat or his truck or on foot. I enjoy our outings because he knows the upper Columbia landscape and main stem valley so well. I like listening to his rambling, engaged narrative. We eat soggy sandwiches, and sometimes there is a beer or two. He once told me he knew where the grave marker was, and how to find it.

Sure, Charlie says to me on the phone tonight. *I'll take you over to Oatscott.*

***

The term *extinction* typically refers to the complete elimination of a species. In the 1950s, the Canadian government also used it for what they call "Indian bands." This is their term for groups of Indians who live on land reserves set aside for their use. The word *band* is not synonymous with "First Nations" (in Canada) or "tribes" (in. the US). It is a bureaucratic word that originated in a time of profound cultural misunderstanding of indigenous people. People were assigned membership in bands, and then told where to live and held there under the colonial belief that Canada's founding cultures were destined either to die off or to be fully assimilated into the dominant settler culture after a few generations of confinement. Government agents created the names and concepts behind Indian bands. Often they had little knowledge of the landscape where tribes had lived and practised their culture; government agents rarely spoke any of the bands' languages. It was all a part of federal Indian policy in which indigenous people were either forcibly or coercively moved to reserves created by the government.

In BC, the process of forming Indian bands began in about 1870. In all but a few cases, the formation of reserves happened without any formal treaties being signed.[10]

***

It's a breezy, almost cloudless summer day when I help Charlie lift his tinner out of his pickup and lower it into the Arrow Lakes reservoir south of Burton. The wind ruffles the surface of water stained a beautiful blue-green by glacial silt flushed down from the high mountains.

Once we are in the water, Charlie muses in his typical, rich fashion as he steers.

Sure, the water is clean and drinkable, right from a cup dipped over the side of the boat. I've done it. But nothing grows here. No duckweed any more. No sedges. Nothing left for the waterfowl to eat. Before Arrow Dam, we had mergansers and pintails, goldeneyes and mallards. All different varieties of geese. I remember them scattering from the shoreline all the time, and in autumn the whole valley was a way station for the birds passing overhead. Herons everywhere. Trumpeter swans. Now that it's a reservoir, geese come to a build a nest in spring and the water rises to flood the nest. The small wetlands and moist back-eddy sloughs all along the river are gone.

Losses on such a grand scale are never immediately apparent. The water glitters persistently in the sunshine. The mountains surrounding it are majestic and inspiring. I scan the shoreline.

---

[10] Duff.

On the survey maps, the seasonally inundated flood plains were marked by blue, sedge-like tufts separated by running dotted lines. They fall under the name "marshes" in the map key – meadows at times overflowing with the blue camas (*Camassia quamash*), a sustaining wild food for the Sinixt people.[11] But the survey maps didn't mention the camas.

No opportunities for seasonal wetlands exist in a reservoir that controls the water levels at the whim of treaties and power production. All around us, the water swells, cool and inviting, but with a uniformity that is lifeless. This water functions for urban and industrial use, not for wild plants and animals, or even for agriculture. Charlie holds the tiller with one hand, pointing with the other to a cut block on a nearby steep mountainside that he created a few years ago for a new hydro line. As we approach the west side of the reservoir, leaves, bits of bark and shreds of wood begin to litter the swells. Last winter was one of deep snow, followed by a spring and early summer of very heavy rain, leading BC Hydro to hold the reservoir especially high for an especially long time.[12] It's still very

---

[11] For more information on camas and its geographic reach in the upper basin, see http://growwild.kics.bc.ca/Articles/KootenayCamasProject/index.htm.

[12] For three weeks starting in early July 2012, the reservoir level climbed to nearly 1,446 feet (440.7 metres), reaching its maximum on July 22. While the CRT determines 1,444 feet (440 metres) as the typical annual high water mark, it also allows the US to draw on two extra feet if necessary for flood control. In the 45-plus years of the CRT, the US has never asked for that increase. In 2012, as spring rains continued and flood threats persisted, Hydro asked the provincial water comptroller for permission to raise the reservoir to 1,447 feet (441 metres) if necessary, to avert flooding in Canada. (Kelvin Ketchum, BC Hydro, personal communication, November 26, 2012.)

high. When we pull the boat in at Oatscott, it is right near the high water mark. I can quickly see that there isn't a hope of seeing the configurations of the old shoreline. With no beach or gradual slope, we must navigate a tangle of freshly fallen trees and soil caving in from the recent extremes. Somewhere underwater is the landscape where a portion of the two dozen original members of the official Arrow Lake Indian Band once erected simple homes and cultivated modest gardens above a sandy beach along what was then the Lower Arrow Lake.

In 1977, Dot Crabbe, a resident of nearby Edgewood, BC, discovered five skeletons. She was out fishing with her husband during the early spring, when reservoir water levels were low, when she saw the exposed remains. Crabbe, herself a registered member of the Colville Confederated Tribes of Washington State, had married a Canadian and lived most of her life above the boundary, not on the American reservation, as she was entitled to do. Her surprise discovery led to the government of BC contacting the Okanagan Indian Band at Head of the Lake in Vernon to oversee a reburial of the remains, since the Arrow Lakes Band was extinct on paper in Canada. Descendants of the Arrow Lakes tribe did exist in the US on the Colville Indian Reservation, but Canadian government policy determined that only Canadian "status" Indians could take care of the remains,[13] which officially eliminated Dot Crabbe from

---

[13] Today, the Canadian federal stance on the Arrow Lakes Indians/ Sinixt reinforces the position that the Arrow Lakes Indian Band and its interests are represented by the Okanagan Nation Alliance, not by the tribal members with status on the US reservation. A connection between the Okanagan Nation Alliance and the Arrow Lakes tribe is the result of marriage bonds between the tribes and of policy decisions in

that process, too. Members of the Vernon Indian Band oversaw the reburial of the remains in the woods above the reservoir, covered by a granite slab funded by BC Hydro.[14]

We scramble up the bank. The most recent big water year has caused even more soil-sloughing than usual, making access to the firm ground above the reservoir's high water mark a real challenge. I slip and fall twice. Exposed sandy soil fills my shoes, and I scrape my shin on fallen timber. Charlie goes down only once. Soon he is standing at the top of the steep bank at the edge of the forest, waiting for me.

* * *

The 1846 international boundary divided both the Columbia River and the traditional territory of the Arrow Lakes/Sinixt people. With the stroke of a diplomatic pen, approximately 20 per cent of their landscape became part of the US, and 80 per cent part of the British territory that was soon to become the Dominion of Canada.[15] The placement of the boundary, and Canada's subsequent delay in setting up an Indian reserve for them north of the border set the stage for extinction and lack of access to more than three-quarters of their territory.

---

the 1950s, when the Department of Indian Affairs attempted to oversee an amalgamation of the Arrow Lakes Band into the Vernon Band of the Okanagan. For more details on contemporary suppression of Arrow Lakes identity, see Geiger.

[14] *Arrow Lakes News,* August 31, 1977. By the early 1950s, only one person on the Indian band roster, Annie Joseph, was still alive. She had left Oatscott many years earlier to be with relatives from the Vernon Band after her husband and sons died. This may explain why the Canadian government chose to contact the Vernon Band to assist with reburial.

[15] Bouchard and Kennedy, *First Nations' Ethnography and Ethnohistory*; Geiger.

After the closure of the trade forts in the 1850s, the US created the Colville Indian Reservation in 1872 and ordered 12 different tribes, including the trans-boundary Arrow Lakes/Sinixt living south of the line, to live within its boundaries. From 1872 to 1890, the US reservation on the west side of the Columbia stretched all the way to the international boundary. In the 1880s, the BC Indian agent charged with creating reserves in Canada took a tour through the region but overlooked or ignored the needs of the Arrow Lakes tribe in the upper Columbia River valley.[16] With no reserve yet in Canada, the Arrow Lakes tribe increasingly spent time on what became known as the "north half" of the reservation, between the Kettle Falls fishery and the 49th parallel, in an area known as Kelly Hill.[17] From here, they could maintain proximity to the "Canadian" portion of their traditional territory. They continued to cross the boundary and to hunt, fish and gather plant foods, especially huckleberries.

In 1891, in response to public pressure, the US government purchased 1.5 million acres from the Colville Confederated Tribe and opened the north half of the reservation to settlement. Many Arrow Lakes people received allotments of land at that time.[18] By 1900, as the area grew more settled, the boundary between the US and Canada was more strictly enforced.[19] With still no reserve for Arrow

---

[16] Geiger.

[17] As late as 1900, an Arrow Lakes/Sinixt chief lived with a village of tribal people on the west shore of the Columbia opposite Northport, Washington, a few miles south of the 49th parallel.

[18] For a detailed account of the closure of the north half of the Colville Indian Reservation, see Arnold.

[19] In the summer of 1898, the *Northport News* reported that customs

Lakes Indians in the Canadian portion of their traditional territory, members of the Arrow Lakes tribe were faced with two difficult options: take an allotment and lose reservation privileges, or relocate further south within the new boundary of the reservation. Either choice isolated them further from most of their traditional territory.

In 1902, the Oatscott Reserve was finally established in Canada, but only after public pressure from non-Indian people.[20] Members of the tribe who still travelled north on a regular basis or lived year-round above the boundary had been promised and were still hoping for a reserve much closer to the international boundary, at a traditional village called *kp'itl'els*, near Castlegar. The Oatscott reserve

---

officers had been searching for some Indians "smuggling" horses across the line. The editor of the paper wrote that he could remember the time "only five years ago" when an American or Indian "could take all the stock he liked across the line and not a question [was] asked. Times have changed so much in the last few years," he concluded, "that the 'old timers' cannot keep track of it, to say nothing about the Indians." The historical record describes Sinixt people crossing the border frequently up to about 1900, timing that correlates with the closure of the north half of the US reservation. Ten miles up the Columbia into Canada, near Beaver Creek, they "built a little willow fence to keep their half dozen or so ponies out of an adjoining meadow which belonged to the owner of the land, and spent a few days hunting." (Graham.) Increased border protection, combined with the relocated boundary of the reservation and new forms of land ownership, made trans-boundary trips of the Sinixt an increasing challenge, though the trips did not abate, according to tribal elders.

[20] For a summary of the efforts of the Christian family and ethnographer James Teit to secure land that had been promised to the Arrow Lakes tribe, see Bouchard and Kennedy, *First Nations' Ethnography and Ethnohistory*.

had no road access, no school and no doctor. It was on marginal land for farming and was not close to a traditional fishery or known traditional villages. To live at Oatscott year-round would mean further isolation from family at Kelly Hill and from those who had moved yet further south to Inchelium, on the Colville Reservation. The original Indian band list at Oatscott reflected the complexity of the situation with just over two dozen members, total. As might be expected given the context, the government Indian agent had to press people to remain in the remote location.[21]

* * *

Once Charlie and I are away from the immediate shoreline and deeper into the woods, things don't improve. There are signs everywhere of a wild windstorm a few weeks earlier, during which 50-to-100-year-old trees tumbled over like matchsticks across the region. With the blow-downs, the forest doesn't look the same to Charlie. We make slow progress, climbing over the rough, grey bark of fallen mature hemlocks and weaving around cedar snags that still smell wet with life. He apologizes that he can't make a straight line for the grave marker. I am simply glad that Charlie is leading.

---

[21] The experience of the Arrow Lakes Indians was not unique. With the exception of the Metis, official Indian identity in Canada today still links to the original Indian band rosters, not to tribal identity or bloodline. Until the 1980s, female band members across Canada lost their legal status if they married outside the band, which happened to some of the women on the Arrow Lakes list. Several young men at Oatscott also succumbed to injury or tuberculosis in the 1920s before having children, further reducing the band's ability to grow. The government determination of membership in an Indian band only through the male line had a significant impact.

Eventually, he spots what he is looking for through the tangle: a low split-rail fence, weathered grey and practically hidden to all but the most trained eye, enclosing about 20 square feet. Inside the fence sits a polished granite slab memorializing all those known to have been buried on the Oatscott Reserve up to 1931, among them Antoine Baptiste, the father and a son of Frank Joseph, Chief Baptiste, his wife, his sons and a daughter, and two unknown people.[22] It is here that the five remains discovered by Dot Crabbe and her husband were also put to rest.

A letter to BC Hydro, dated May 23, 1961, from H.T. Ramsden of Vancouver, district engineer for the federal Department of Northern Affairs and National Resources, states that according to Ramsden's information, "no Indian Reserves or graveyards would be affected by the [proposed] High Arrow Project on the Columbia River near Castlegar."[23] Another letter, dated the following year, from Ottawa's Department of Indian Affairs to the Indian commissioner for BC, indicates an awareness of graves but states that "no good purpose can be served to have these graves relocated above the proposed flooded area."[24] By early 1968, a BC Hydro official appeared to be informed of at least four graves "on the west shore of the Lower Arrow Lake, north of Needles BC" (approximately the location of Oatscott). In the letter, R.C. McMordie, Columbia projects manager, proposes to "move the graves to a cemetery in the area because we

---

[22] Mohs, *Post-Inundation Archaeological Survey*, and personal communication, August 2012.

[23] H.T. Ramsden to W.J. McGregor, May 23, 1961, Department of Northern Affairs and National Resources file no. 2049-802.

[24] H.M. Jones to J.V. Boys, August 22, 1962, Department of Indian Affairs file no. 1/8-4-1(r.8) 164/30-7 DV/vp.

consider the reservoir banks at their present location may become unstable during the reservoir operations."[25] Whether these particular graves were relocated is not clear. What is clear is that some graves were not protected at all. This led to Dot Crabbe's discovery in the 1970s, and many others since then. A report on salvage archaeology conducted about the time of her discovery determined that 90 per cent of archaeological sites in the Arrow Lakes valley had been flooded and destroyed by the storage reservoirs.[26]

Charlie and I lean against the log fence and watch shafts of summer sunlight reach through the trees to strike the polished granite slab. I pull out two sandwiches. While we eat, we both notice that there are no blow-downs within 50 yards of the fenced burials. It's as if all these years and so many misunderstandings later, the remains are finally being protected. We sit in silence as the forest shifts and rustles around us.

Today, legal identity for any Arrow Lakes/Sinixt person in Canada remains dependent on the Indian Band roster established over a century ago with two dozen names. This government policy keeps several thousand Arrow Lakes people from experiencing their aboriginal right to their territory, one that history confirms is legitimate.

At the time of the Canadian extinction of the Arrow Lakes Indian Band, several hundred members of the Arrow Lakes tribe were living on the Colville Reservation, or off-reservation on the private allotments in the former "north half" between the Sounding Waters fishery and the boundary. More were on reserves set aside

---

[25] R.C. McMordie, Columbia Projects Manager, BC Hydro, to John McGregor, Indian Affairs (Vancouver), January 29, 1968.
[26] Mohs.

for neighbouring Indian bands in Canada, having joined relations living there who had status under the Indian Act. Some of these people and their descendants have continued to journey north into Canada, or west and east from other Canadian reserves to pick huckleberries, hunt and fish in the traditional territory of the Arrow Lakes people. All of them have retained an understanding of their cultural homeland on the upper Columbia River in Canada.

The extinction and subsequent erasure of Arrow Lakes Indian cultural history from the main stem of the Columbia was part of a larger process related to the international water treaty. The CRT was all about the future, not the past. It was all about preparing the entire landscape for de-inhabitation. In the inevitable disconnection of people from place that results from hydro-electric megaprojects, the archaeological heritage of the people was neglected, then destroyed. Storage reservoirs provide the resilient supply of year-round electricity that customers demand. But they are destructive of natural river systems and their human history.

Charlie and I weave back through the forest to the boat and set out on the water again, headed a few miles upstream to the mouth of Fern Creek. After we beach his tinner, Charlie wanders past me, staying close to a narrow strip of dry gravel that rests above high water, explaining that he and other collectors have found as many as three dozen pounders on this beach, exposed by the operation of the reservoir.[27] Knowing his success on previous visits, he searches along the surface of the silt with a well-practised mixture

---

[27] These 15-to-20-centimetre-long (six-to-eight-inch) granite cylinders from five to ten centimetres (two to four inches) in diameter were an everyday tool used to prepare berries, nuts and dried meat for storage through long winters.

of compulsion and idleness. It's illegal to dig for artifacts in British Columbia, but anyone can wander reservoir shorelines or cutbanks and have a close look.

I crouch in the silt and gaze across the expansive reservoir. On the opposite shore, a steep bluff looms, bisected by a blasted cutaway for the new road constructed in 1968, as the reservoir began to fill. An intricate pictograph painted on this bluff was well known to locals and had been included in the archaeological survey conducted by Peter Harrison for BC Hydro in 1960. In the spring of that year, a resident noticed that work progressing on the new road was advancing toward the pictograph site. She wrote to BC Highways minister P.A. Gaglardi to alert him to the pictograph and ask for it to be preserved. Gaglardi replied that he would take it into consideration. A few months later, blasting for the road completely destroyed the pictograph. When Nelson Museum director Burnie Fetterley visited the location, he found a heap of rubble, with some chunks as big as cars, and no sign of the rock face. The Royal BC Museum confirmed that no permit had been issued, nor were there any fines under the 1961 Archaeology Act, a policy intended to "convince not convict."[28]

Peter Harrison's 1961 government archaeological survey report described the panel in detail: 12 feet by 12 feet and 40 feet above the old road surface. At least ten feet above the nearest ledge, the panel likely required a scaffold for access when it was created. Harrison's report indicated that several of the images were vivid and noticeable from the road, having been retouched by a member of the Arrow Lakes Indian Band in the 1920 and 1930s.[29]

---

[28] *Arrow Lakes News,* June 12, 1968.

[29] Corner. According to Harrison, the pictographs were retouched by Louie Joseph.

According to the 1956 survey maps, the river once narrowed considerably a few miles upstream of Oatscott. Right about here. At low water in autumn, the time of the annual caribou rut, an arrow-shaped sand bar called Caribou Point formed on the shore opposite. Early settlers watched the Sinixt drive caribou into the water on that side. Less than a thousand feet would have separated the east and west sides of the Columbia. This side could very likely have been a processing centre for winter meat supplies, a possible explanation for the large number of stone pounders found here by various collectors over the years.[30] As the men drove the animals into the water and speared them, women would have been hard at work, too: receiving the caribou out of the water, gutting them, processing the hides and slicing the meat away from the bone with sharp slivers archaeologists call micro-blades.[31] Large fires dried the meat before the women ground it into the traditional ststa, or "hammered food," a mixture of bear fat, dried caribou and dried fruit packed into animal intestines for winter storage.

Charlie's voice brings me back.

---

[30] The historical record shows that several early settlers witnessed the practice of deer or caribou drives by the Arrow Lakes tribe. See Bouchard and Kennedy, *First Nations' Ethnography and Ethnohistory,* for details. On April 21, 1827, botanist David Douglas stopped near Fern Creek on a journey upstream to purchase snowshoes for the trek over the Great Divide. In the Arrow Lakes/Sinixt lodge, he saw no fewer than 100 prepared skins of the mountain caribou.

[31] The widespread use of micro-blades dates from two periods: around 10,000 to 12,000 years ago, during the Paleoindian phase, immediately after the glaciers melted back, and more recently, 1200 to 200 years ago. Micro-blades are most commonly obsidian but can be made from good quality chert or fine-grained volcanic rock such as andesite or dacite. (Dr. Nathan Goodale, personal communication, December 11, 2014.)

Check it out, Eileen.

His eyes are wide with disbelief as he holds up an eight-inch triangular slab of stone, about an inch thick with smoothed edges: a schist paddle maul.[32]

I found it here, lying right on the surface.

A set of less experienced eyes might have dismissed the unique paddle maul as a mere slab of rock. Not Charlie. As we pull the boat back into the water, he hands me a cold beer and grins widely.

It's always worth coming out, Eileen, even if you don't find something. He takes a long sip from his beer. *But it's better when you do.*

We putt slowly across the water, my mind playing with words. *Schist – shift – schist – shift – schist.* A schist paddle maul exposed by the operation of the reservoir. A striking shift in values.

Before the landscape could be used for water storage, it had to be precisely known. It had to be measured, qualified, quantified and understood. The 1956 survey maps recorded and preserved the texture of the natural river valley but were also weapons for its profound transformation. The knowledge gathered into the maps fascinates the historian in me, and also feeds my imagination. It helps me piece together the story of the river as it once was. Yet these maps can only hint at the rhythms of a very different time, now submerged by millions of acre-feet of CRT storage.

---

[32] The paddle maul is a tool unique to the upper Columbia, used to tenderize edible black tree lichen (*Bryoria fremontii*) before it was wrapped in leaves and pit-cooked with berries or roots. Schist is a common rock form in the upper Columbia.

Give and Take: Who Made the CRT Decisions and How

1. The Long Road to Libby

In 1957, Montreal Engineering Company released a detailed plan for the hydro-development of the upper Columbia region as part of a contract with the Canadian government. Included in their design for hydro-development – and running contrary to McNaughton's position on water sovereignty – was the Libby Dam, the same project the US had lobbied for unsuccessfully over the previous half a dozen years.[1] Also included was a dam that the engineering firm

---

[1] McNaughton responded decisively to the proposal: "We have no Canadian interests to be served by more storage in this [High Arrow's] location." However, national political changes had altered his status. He was a Liberal party member, but the Liberals no longer held a majority government; now they formed the opposition to a minority Conservative government, which may have dimmed his influence. In the spring of 1958, Canada elected a majority Conservative government led by John Diefenbaker, and prominent Liberals such as McNaughton became even less powerful.

calculated would provide 7.1 MAF of water storage: High Arrow Dam. Positioned just below the southern end of the lower of the two Arrow Lakes (near Castlegar, BC), the storage dam was described as "the most productive project that could be undertaken as an initial stage to serve the power needs of both countries."[2] Ironically, the High Arrow Dam design did not include generators.[3] The electrical productivity for Canada would come from a 50 per cent share of US power efficiencies downstream. This share, referred to as the "downstream benefits" or "Canadian Entitlement," would be returned north of the boundary as power for use or sale. Storage close to the boundary on the Columbia's main stem gave maximum flexibility to the Americans for power generation. This advantage would pass to Canada through the share of downstream benefits. According to the report, Libby Dam could also provide advantages in flood control and water storage for both countries on the Kootenay River system.[4]

In early July 1958, IJC chair McNaughton led an international delegation through the entire Columbia basin from the headwaters to the mouth.[5] At the end of July, Premier Bennett proposed a top-

---

[2] Swainson, 87.

[3] The proposed High Arrow Dam was what hydrologists call a "low head" dam, meaning that its modest height made gravity-flow power generation either impossible or economically inefficient.

[4] This hydro-development would involve construction of a canal around the projects already operated by West Kootenay Power and Light, and installation of a sizable generator at the base of this canal, to be known as the Kootenay Canal Plant.

[5] Asked during a stop in Nelson about the personal relations between the Americans and Canadians in the delegation, McNaughton replied: "We in Canada are sure now of the type of agreement we need. What

level conference between Eisenhower, Diefenbaker and himself to facilitate an agreement on how the CRT projects might be financed, even though they had not yet been chosen. The deal Bennett had made with Kaiser had been scuttled, but he was continuing to strategize about how he could get industry and the federal government to pay for provincial hydro-development. The federal government declined on the grounds that the matter should be left with the Department of External Affairs, and should wait until the IJC Engineering Board report was released.[6] Late that same year, a federally appointed Committee on Economic Studies of Columbia River Development released a confidential report analyzing the economic aspects of various proposals. The report sided with General McNaughton's preferences. Storage from a High Arrow Dam was considered in only one alternative. Libby Dam was included in none of them.[7]

* * *

It takes me nearly three hours to descend from the moist thicket of forest in the heart of the Selkirk Mountains to the arid Rocky Mountain Trench. I want to see Libby Dam, the contentious project at the heart of the CRT negotiations. I pull into Cranbrook, still nearly three hours away from the dam. From Canada, the road to Libby is a long one.

Operated by the US Army Corps of Engineers, Libby Dam is out of sight and mind to most Canadians, even though it has a

---

instructions the American Commissioners have ... and what future pressure they might get I cannot say." (*Nelson Daily News,* July 23, 1958.)

[6] Swainson, 92–93.

[7] Swainson, 98–99.

significant ecological impact on Kootenay Lake, the entire Kootenay River and all its tributaries. Many Americans have a similar myopia about where the Kootenay River goes when it exits the dam in western Montana. The water that originated in Canada heads east to Idaho, then north again across the border, flowing through Kootenay Lake and west through the lake's arm and lower river before joining up with the main stem of the Columbia and heading south into the US again. The dam's trans-boundary design and complex function forms an important hub in the CRT story. The dam exists because of political power struggles between the US and Canada, between Canada's federal government and BC's provincial leaders, and between agricultural and industrial communities within the upper Columbia region itself.

**

W.A.C. Bennett was focused on fulfilling his provincial goal of completing projects as quickly as he could, with as little fiscal impact as possible, but continued to meet with resistance from the federal government about the financing of the CRT dams. The federal government was most interested in creating a cooperative plan that maximized international harmony. Impatient, Bennett charged ahead that autumn with a new set of plans – to develop a hydro-electric project on the Peace River. Since the Peace River was not international like the Columbia, it was not subject to federal involvement.[8] He announced another partnership with private

---

[8] When announcing an agreement with the Wenner-Gren Company to construct a hydro-electric dam on the Peace River, Bennett said: "Surely now both Ottawa and the US will realize we mean business ... the development of B.C. won't be held back while the US and Ottawa hold pink teas." (Quoted in Swainson, 84.)

industry, this time with the Wenner-Gren Company. Bennett's vision was to harness hydro-power on the Peace and the Columbia together – his Two Rivers Policy. His ambitious goal influenced the negotiations between Canada and the US.

Early in 1959, Crippen-Wright Engineering tabled its own report. Hired by the BC provincial government, Crippen-Wright recommended High Arrow as the first and most beneficial project on the main stem, assuming that a favourable agreement could be reached to share downstream benefits with the Americans.[9] The report did not recommend extensive diversion and damming on the Kootenay River in the Rocky Mountain Trench, as McNaughton had proposed, in part due to the destructive impact on wildlife and the disruption to a transportation corridor 150 miles long. The High Arrow storage-only dam described by Crippen-Wright would inundate nearly 6,000 acres of farmland and a total of 100,000 acres, as well as disrupt a 60-year-old ferry system serving many communities.[10] In reference to this upheaval, the report said only that there was a need "to establish provincial policy on the flooding of valleys."[11]

In March 1959, a third report on potential development of the upper Columbia was released: the long-awaited recommendations

---

[9] After High Arrow, Crippen-Wright recommended, in order, the following projects: a Kootenay Canal generating plant on the lower Kootenay River, a dam/generator at Seven Mile on the Pend-d'Oreille River, a storage dam at Mica (with generators added later), Revelstoke Canyon dam/generators and Downie Creek dam/generators. The Downie Creek project was cancelled due to concerns over slope stability.

[10] *Valley Voice,* March 20, 2013.

[11] Quoted in Swainson, 105.

of the Columbia River Engineering Study Group of the IJC. Their recommendations added to the jumble of possibilities emerging from various consultants. The study group laid out several possible sequences reflecting a decade and a half of discussion, but did not offer a preference. Another, shorter report from the IJC discussed equitable division of advantages from the treaty. This report was prepared in response to a request from both national governments. In it, the IJC stated the importance of ensuring that any plan shared advantages equally. It stressed the benefits of sharing the generated power rather than money.[12]

As 1959 ended, both countries moved closer to political treaty negotiations, but still no firm preference for one plan over another emerged. Meanwhile, Bennett had realized that if he was to achieve his ambitious Two Rivers Policy, the province needed the federal government to pick up the tab for the Columbia project. At this point, Bennett may or may not have yet thought about converting downstream benefits from the Columbia hydro-development into cash to finance the CRT dams. In early December 1959, he wrote pointedly to Ottawa, asking again for their views on how the CRT projects should be financed.

Engineering personnel advising the federal government felt that the construction of High Arrow would confer maximum economic benefits. Some federal elected officials and senior bureaucrats appeared to have had grave concerns about the political costs of

---

[12] IJC, *Report of the International Joint Commission, United States and Canada on Principles for Determining and Apportioning Benefits from Cooperative Use of the Storage of Waters and Electrical Inter-Connection within the Columbia River System.*

displacing up to 2,000 residents in the Arrow Lakes valley.[13] For his part, McNaughton, as an advocate for Canadian water sovereignty, continued to argue that the case for High Arrow's economic value was based too heavily on the value of the downstream benefits. These, he insisted, would decline over time as other power sources came on stream (nuclear and coal were planned), thus neutralizing what he saw at the time as a short-term economic benefit to the High Arrow Dam.[14]

***

I leave Cranbrook and head east to catch up with the Kootenay River as it flows through the Rocky Mountain Trench toward Montana. It isn't raining yet, although a storm is definitely building across the broad western sky, with jostling clouds that echo my impatience. The brief and proximate parallel span of these rivers once caused great confusion to the explorer David Thompson as he searched for the Columbia in 1807. Not realizing that the Columbia would go north for a few hundred miles before turning south again at the Big Bend, Thompson encountered the Kootenay flowing south through the trench and followed it, thinking that this was the great river indigenous chiefs had told him flowed south and west to the ocean.[15] Instead, the Kootenay River guided him into the steep, rocky canyons of western Montana.

---

[13] Swainson, 115.

[14] In fact, nuclear and coal sources did not materialize as expected. The downstream benefits grew more valuable over time.

[15] For more on Thompson's confusion, see Nisbet.

In 1842, during his journey around the world, Hudson's Bay Company governor George Simpson followed in Thompson's footsteps, travelling along the broad Rocky Mountain trench, which he described as "a prairie lying along the Kootennais [Kootenay], which bore a considerable resemblance to a fine park." Simpson remarked on how the trees formed "grand avenues," almost as if they had been planted that way.[16] The highway I am on cuts a diagonal line through the remnants of Simpson's graceful pine forest, joining the Kootenay River near Wardner, BC. Wardner is the northernmost Canadian community that was permanently flooded and destroyed by Libby's trans-boundary Koocanusa reservoir.

***

With the dispute growing between the Canadian federal and provincial governments about how to finance the proposed CRT storage projects,[17] representatives of the US, Canada and BC began official treaty negotiations behind closed doors in Washington and Ottawa. General Andrew McNaughton, despite his experience and proven strength as a bargainer on the IJC, was not invited to sit at the table. Davie Fulton, federal minister of foreign affairs and as such lead negotiator for Canada, was generally supportive of a sovereign plan for water. His public statements leading up to the start

---

[16] The ponderosa pine savannah Simpson so admired was the product of thousands of years of low-intensity forest fires, a common occurrence before government fire suppression. Indigenous cultures on the Interior Plateau have record of controlled burning to facilitate root and berry crops.

[17] For precise details on how the federal government moved forward on their negotiation strategy in late 1959 and early 1960 without having resolved the conflict with Bennett, see Swainson, 121–25.

of the negotiation's first phase expressed little enthusiasm for Libby Dam or for the storage-only project of High Arrow. The outcome of discussions was still unknown, but from Canada's perspective, things were tilting toward a more extensive sovereign development for hydro-power production, as McNaughton envisioned, including a diversion of the Kootenay River into the Columbia. This position stood in direct opposition to W.A.C. Bennett's developing vision to finance the CRT dams with a lump sum from downstream benefits.

Throughout 1960, negotiators positioned and bargained. The Americans were keen to construct Libby, especially for the flood control it would offer to the agricultural community in Bonners Ferry, Idaho; they were also anxious to achieve their storage needs for Columbia River power efficiencies. Canadian negotiators expressed reservations about giving too much capacity to the US, especially in terms of Libby's control of the Kootenay River, a river that originated in BC. Provincial representatives from BC were leaning toward measuring the benefit of the various options based on short-term economic needs. Bennett remained fixated on financing the CRT projects so that the Peace River project could be developed at the same time.[18]

Private industry on both sides of the boundary voiced the benefits of cooperative storage as financially beneficial to the US and potentially lucrative for BC.[19] Industry representatives based in Trail, BC,

---

[18] For a full discussion of the first phase of treaty negotiations, especially related to project selection, see Swainson, 121–56.

[19] A consortium of private business interests on both sides of the border calling itself the Canadian-American Committee weighed in with its opinions in a jointly produced informational pamphlet entitled *Cooperative Development of the Columbia River Basin.*

strongly supported Libby Dam because of the enhancement of hydro-power production on the lower Kootenay River that it would offer. In the agriculture sector, there was less unity. High Arrow Dam, were it chosen, would flood the entire Arrow Lakes valley, along with over a dozen communities, and destroy the agricultural life there. Libby Dam appealed to farmers in Creston, BC, as flood control. Residents of the Rocky Mountain Trench near the Columbia's headwaters did not want to see McNaughton's vision realized, given the devastating impact large projects in that valley would have on headwaters wildlife and transportation. The conflict between these groups came to a head during a controversial meeting of chambers of commerce of southeastern BC early in 1960.[20]

Co-chaired by Robert M. Fowler, president of the Canadian Pulp and Paper Association and R. Douglas Stuart, chair of the board of the Quaker Oats Company, the committee argued that Canadian storage "can produce exceptionally low-cost power" by enhancing the function of facilities that already existed in the US. This, the committee said, would cost much less than creating entirely new facilities in the US, or in Canada, for that matter. The committee urged an emphasis on economic potential in order to keep the negotiations from "becoming obscured by engineering, legal and political intricacies."

[20] Guy Constable of Creston, J.D. McMynn of Trail and F.E. Coy of Invermere (representatives from the water resources committee of the Associated Chambers of Commerce of Southeastern BC) published a report supporting the High Arrow project for the "strong bargaining" position it would give Canada in negotiating with the United States on downstream benefits. When the meeting of associated chambers began, delegates from the Arrow Lakes valley demanded that the report be thrown out, claiming that the regional committee was "selling our heritage" with its recommendations. When pressed, McMynn and Constable admitted that they had originally favoured a low dam at Murphy Creek for its reduced local impact, but a recent meeting with

At the centre of the controversy was lands and forests minister Ray Williston, who, after the meeting, issued a statement claiming that the provincial government had not yet decided on the final plan for development of the Columbia and that the "Kootenays have the power and resources and should be the first to benefit." He went on to promise that no water licence for the CRT projects would be granted without proper public hearings, adding that the "people of the Kootenays are the ones vitally concerned and they are entitled to be heard."[21]

Negotiations were nearly completed, yet no meetings or formal consultation with residents or their representatives had yet occurred in the region. Despite Williston's promises, no specific plans emerged for how to consult with residents about the various options.

* * *

I carry on past the flooded community of Jaffray and veer east to hook up with Highway 93. This direct path to the boundary means that I will bypass some important history submerged beneath the Libby reservoir: the lost places of Big Sand Creek, Waldo, Krag, Elkmouth, Dorr, Flagstone and Newgate. Situated in the traditional territory of the Tobacco Plains Band of the Ktunaxa Nation (Kootenai Tribe in the US), the flooded land had been inhabited before settlement by Chief David and his Tobacco Plains–Ktunaxa people. Chief David had asked the Canadian government to set

---

provincial minister Ray Williston and his advisors had convinced them to change their minds. In the end, the associated chambers approved the report, but only once the specific recommendation of the High Arrow plan had been removed. (*Nelson Daily News*, January 25, 1960.)

[21] *Nelson Daily News*, January 26, 1960.

aside the vast river-valley bottomland as reserve. Instead, he was given only 10,531 acres for the use of his people – a marginal strip of land running along the foot of the Rocky Mountains from Grasmere to the international boundary.[22]

I cross the boundary just east of the Kootenay River at Roosville, BC, still puzzling over the geographic anomaly that means an American dam *south* of the line floods Canadian land *north* of it. As I drive south and slightly west toward the dam, the landscape around me shifts again. I am moving away from the arid, open terrain of the Rocky Mountain Trench and its sparse, gracious pines back to a denser, more varied mix of conifers and steeper, rocky canyons. Rain clouds loom large as I lay my tires against the centre-line of the narrow highway hewn into the cliffs.

At last, in the distance, I see a thin line of concrete and the pooled water gathered behind it, forming two shades of grey, robed in the overcast light. A splendid blond stone tower rises midway across the grey crest, forming a sharp contrast to the black rain clouds. Then the road curves, and I lose sight of the dam. When I finally see it again, I am nearly beside it. I pull into a parking lot marked by an innocuous brown sign: *Libby Dam.*

---

[22] In 1887, Major Peter O'Reilly, superintendent of Indian reserves in BC, met with Chief David to discuss possible reserve lands. When asked to choose, the chief asked for all the land between the Rockies and Purcells, from the mouth of the Elk River south to the international boundary. O'Reilly suspended the meeting until the following day but departed without further discussion. Government surveyors later arrived when the chief's band was away hunting and marked out a fraction of the land requested, ordering the tribe to live within the boundaries. For more details, see Wedemeyer.

***

At some point in 1960, the BC negotiators began to push hard for the High Arrow Dam, realizing that the generous amount of downstream benefits translated into a lump-sum cash payment could provide greater liquidity. This was the "first added" advantage of High Arrow's storage, located near the boundary, where it could be most accessible for American use. In a twist on McNaughton's vision for equal sharing of benefits, BC had perceived that benefits from storage behind High Arrow, if sold to the US in a lump sum in advance, could provide the cash to finance the construction of the CRT dams. As negotiations continued, the position for Canada's water sovereignty, built slowly by McNaughton through his insistence on the right to divert the flow of rivers that originated in Canada, began to shift under the weight of BC interests in project financing. An immediately profitable plan emerged.

In autumn of 1960, W.A.C. Bennett called an election to receive a fresh mandate, with the campaign slogan "Vote for the Government that Gets Things Done." No details about the CRT negotiations had been released to the public, but it was evident to many in provincial politics that the choice of a High Arrow Dam was, at this point, a foregone conclusion.[23] On September 12, 1960, BC went to the polls. When the night was over, Bennett's government had reduced its majority but still had a mandate. In October, the US and Canada released a progress report on negotiations for the cooperative

---

[23] Swainson, 162.

development of the Columbia River, indicating that both Libby
Dam and the High Arrow projects had been chosen to form the
base for an international treaty.[24]

At this point, BC had still not initiated any formal consultation
with residents in the affected area. When residents of the Arrow
Lakes valley read the report, they contacted Minister Williston,
who once again stood as the primary intermediary between the
local people and those involved in government negotiations. He
assured residents in an October letter that as a part of the formal
process of application for water licences, "public hearings will
be held in the areas affected." And then, very clearly, he said that
only after provincial water licences were granted would "the way
be open for the two federal governments to proceed to treaty
negotiations."[25] Back in Ottawa in late November, Williston passed

---

[24] American capital outlay for storage *without* Canadian assistance was
estimated to cost $710-million. With High Arrow and the two other
Canadian storage dams in place, the same increase in power capacity
would cost the US only $410-million. "Availability of this power," the
document explained, "will give time to resolve local problems of the
effect of dam and reservoir construction in critical areas in the United
States on fish and wildlife." The report also described the positive
impact on "more uniformly regulated flows" on the lower portions of
the Columbia due to Canadian storage, in terms of both navigation
and irrigation. The primary benefit for Canada, though it is not clear
from reading this document, was the high monetary value of the power
being returned as "downstream benefits." This reward was considered
sufficient for the cost and disruption of constructing the dams, though
some Canadian analysts believed that the costs of construction had
been underestimated. (Swainson, 169.) The impact on Canadian fish and
wildlife, the loss of Canadian farmland and the displacement of over
2,000 residents were factors not mentioned in the analysis of costs.

[25] Quoted in Waterfield, *Continental Waterboy.*

on his concerns about the treaty, naming and entrenching specific projects. He reminded negotiators in Ottawa that, as part of provincial resource development practices, the treaty could not be finalized before public hearings for the water licence.

Based on the events that followed, his concerns appear to have fallen on deaf ears. Negotiators were more concerned about the fact that US President Eisenhower had not been re-elected. Both countries worried about starting negotiations at square one with a new government. A sense of urgency to complete the process began to override other issues.[26]

Meanwhile, the game of poker between the federal and provincial governments in Canada continued. On October 26, 1960, W.A.C. Bennett wrote again to the federal government, asking two blunt questions: How much were the feds prepared to grant to the Province of BC to construct the dams, and how much were they prepared to lend? Bennett did not appear concerned about the residents of the Arrow Lakes valley. He was still hoping to work out a way to finance construction of both the Peace project and the Columbia development at the same time.[27]

---

[26] Swainson, 173.

[27] According to *The Vancouver Sun*, the federal government replied to Bennett's pointed questions in a letter dated October 27, 1960: they would provide one-half of the estimated $344-million in capital cost of the storage projects. The funds would be an investment in a joint federal-provincial project. In a series of further questions, Bennett requested clarification of details including the interest rate the government would charge, the terms of a loan, and whether or not the federal government would require the government of BC to guarantee the loan. He was not pleased that there was no offer for an outright grant to fund the Columbia dams.

* * *

From the roadside lookout above the dam, I can only see a few miles upstream. The view cannot allow me to perceive the geographic U-turn that results in Libby Dam's unique situation: both Canada and the US are downstream of each other in the Kootenay River drainage. I cross the deserted parking lot to a gate in the chain-link fence that bars entrance to a walkway across the dam's crest. The gate is locked. Since the terrorist attacks of September 11, 2001, security measures around dams have tightened. Once trumpeted as a draw for tourists, walkways across dam crests are now strictly off limits.

Libby is to some people a handsome dam. The Army Corps of Engineers hired a Seattle architect, Paul Thiry, to flesh out the details of its design. The Corps wanted a dam that was publicly appealing but not too costly – megaprojects were being regarded with increasing suspicion at the time.[28] The construction of Libby, a gravity dam spanning a rock canyon nearly 915 metres (3,000 feet) wide, required the same amount of concrete as a two-lane highway from New York to Salt Lake City.[29]

On the downstream wall, facing Canada, is a bas-relief sculpture created by New York sculptor Albert Wein. It depicts a muscular indigenous man, arms spread wide to block the path of two wild horses; a few Canada geese fly in the air beside him, and two fish swim below in calm water. The sculpture was supposed to stand as a monument of international cooperation. In reality, however, there

[28] Van Huizen.
[29] Spritzer.

was enough international awkwardness about the project by the time of its dedication in 1973 that Canada's prime minister, along with several other Canadian officials, declined to attend alongside then-US president Gerald Ford. W.A.C. Bennett's government had been replaced in 1972, and the new BC premier, Dave Barrett, was threatening to divert what water he could from the Kootenay under the terms of the CRT.[30]

***

On December 8, 1960, with less than two months remaining before John F. Kennedy was sworn in as the new president, federal and provincial negotiators gathered with more urgency, to hammer out the final details of the treaty so that Eisenhower could sign it. Bennett had received a clear reply to his question about financing the projects, and it was apparently not to his liking. Still intent on fulfilling his Two Rivers Policy, still annoyed by the federal incursion into his management of BC's resource development dating back to 1954, he did not appreciate the latest federal offer of a financing package that would have the province owing interest back to the federal government for the money offered for construction of the projects.

The following day, *The Vancouver Sun* reported on a meeting between Bennett and federal representative Davie Fulton: "Bennett, Fulton Exchange Hot Words on River Issue." The justice minister and the provincial premier called independent news conferences at which they challenged each other's positions. Bennett openly rejected the federal financing proposal, claiming that it had too many strings attached. Fulton insisted that Bennett was

---

[30] Ibid.

misrepresenting the substance of the proposal. He claimed that if the Columbia Treaty process bogged down further, any delay would rest at the feet of the Province of BC. In reply, Bennett was characteristically independent and bold. BC would, he said, finance the entire $458-million cost of the dams by itself, if necessary.

"The nature and terms of Premier Bennett's response establish clearly he had made up his mind to reject it for political purposes," Fulton said. "We are not prepared to allow the benefits accruing under this treaty to be sold for cash which would go into the province's general revenues and be used for financing other pet projects of the premier of BC." Bennett responded that the federal position effectively removed "control of that resource from this province." Fulton complained to reporters that on several occasions during treaty negotiations, federal members of a policy committee had attempted to discuss finance details with BC members, but the premier had forbidden it.[31]

The clock was ticking as the bickering continued. Back in Ottawa on December 13, Justice Minister Fulton announced in the House of Commons that the federal government would go ahead with treaty negotiations despite being at loggerheads on how to finance the project. December arrived, and the inability of the province to reach an agreement with the federal government about how the projects would be financed presented a stark contrast to American eagerness to get the treaty signed before President Eisenhower left office in January.

The new year began with no resolution in sight to the financing dispute between the province and the federal government. On January 4, the *Calgary Herald* reported that "the federal government

---

[31] *The Vancouver Sun*, December 9, 1960.

is caught in the middle – between the Americans who want to proceed, and the provincial side which appears to be holding out, perhaps for more generous treatment in the financing of the Columbia project." W.A.C. Bennett was saying openly and consistently that he expected an outright grant from the federal government, not an interest-bearing loan. The Eisenhower administration continued to pressure the Canadian government to sign the treaty.

On January 13, Bennett sent a letter to the federal government, stressing his desire to start on the Columbia River projects "at the earliest possible moment." The letter included a warning qualifier: the treaty projects must prove feasible in terms of engineering *and* finances. Bennett made specific reference to the electricity rate at which the downstream benefits might be sold.[32] A clear sign of the still-unresolved differences between the federal and provincial governments, the letter did not appear to reach the key government advisors or Prime Minister Diefenbaker prior to their departure for Washington, DC, to sign the treaty. On January 17, 1961, not having read Premier Bennett's warning letter, Diefenbaker signed the international Columbia River Treaty with Eisenhower.

Bennett considered the letter to have been delivered, and the warning it contained to be one that Ottawa had ignored. The federal government claimed to have been the victim of sharp practice.[33]

* * *

I shake the gate to the crest of the dam a few times. Its lonely clatter joins up with the agitated wind. I follow the chain link fence to

---

[32] *Nelson Daily News* , May 27, 1961.

[33] Swainson, 185.

the edge of the cliff, lean against it and look down. Far below, the reservoir heaves in a slate-grey mass. Suddenly, a fresh, sharp gust of wind whips my sweater into a tangle. A moment later, a bolt of lightning pierces the reservoir surface and a deafening clap of thunder drives me away from the fence. Trembling, I crouch at the base of a concrete abutment. Before I can catch my breath, another fork strikes the water. Rain begins to fall in fat, noisy drops, but I am unable to move. Then a third charge strikes over the water, this one half a mile upstream.

I stumble back to the car through the thickening rain.

***

Immediately after the treaty signing, the *Tri-City Herald* in Washington State reported that Elmer F. Bennett, under-secretary of the interior and a member of the US negotiating team, had detailed the great economic advantages of the treaty for the United States, saying that the country had, for only $402-million, gained water storage that would have cost some $710-million had they built their own projects for that purpose.

The signed CRT authorized the construction in Canada of Duncan and High Arrow dams for flood control. Mica would store water primarily for power generation, once generators were installed at a later date. The first two storage dams were to be completed within five years, Mica within nine. The treaty's payments from the US for flood control in perpetuity were tied to the completion of each of the three dams, with the US$64.4-million portioned between the projects. Despite Mica Dam's significant capacity for storing water, its portion of the flood control payments was only $1.2-million. Arrow, on the other hand, had been apportioned $52.1-million: its

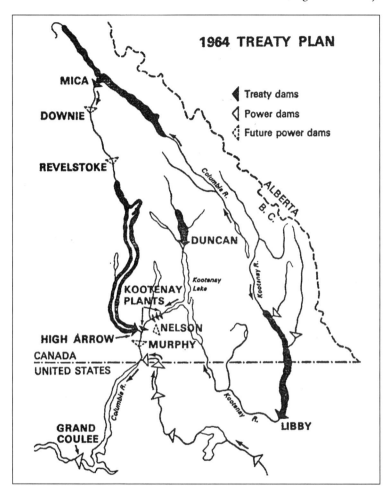

This map shows the CRT's proposed development of the Columbia River, marking existing dams in both countries, the treaty-related projects (High Arrow/Keenleyside, Mica, Duncan and Libby) as well as future hydro power projects (Downie, Revelstoke, Kootenay Canal and Murphy). Of the latter projects, only Revelstoke and Kootenay Canal were completed. FROM WATERFIELD, *CONTINENTAL WATERBOY*.

contributions were considered most favourable in monetary terms, due to its position as one of the first-added projects. The construction deadlines were tight, reflecting a keen American interest in generating more power as quickly as possible, to serve a growing industrial base in the Pacific Northwest. Also written into the treaty was the option for the US Army Corps of Engineers to construct Libby Dam, as long as they began the project within five years. Canada's right to divert Kootenay River water was severely restricted. Canada would be in charge of clearing and preparing land to be flooded along the Kootenay River above the boundary.

The Montreal *Gazette* ran a story soon after the announcement, indicating "a note of warning" from member of Parliament H.W. Herridge, "whose own home will disappear in the rising waters produced by High Arrow Dam." The increased power efficiency and flood control had come at an agreeable economic price. The social, environmental and longer-term economic costs were just emerging from the political mist.

After the signing, Bennett sent a private, double-registered letter to Prime Minister Diefenbaker, explaining that BC was still committed to the Columbia project, but only upon conditions not agreed to as yet.[34] With the construction of the High Arrow Dam now written into the treaty and a new imperative to complete the project, Bennett's continued intractability was beginning to put real pressure on the Canadian federal government to change their position on downstream benefits.

In the tangle of international, national and provincial politics, the Columbia River Engineering Study Group's conclusions – that

---

[34] Mitchell.

Canada should develop as much power-generating potential as possible, and as high up the system as possible – had been swept aside. The treaty had given away Canada's right to divert its own Kootenay River water, protected until then under the Boundary Waters Treaty. While the concept of downstream benefits had survived, McNaughton's principled recommendation that these benefits remain always in the form of raw power was gradually being subverted by a very different and, some would say, equally grand vision – Bennett's idea of developing the Peace and the Columbia concurrently and using the advanced proceeds from one plan to finance the other. Water and the trade of water projects were entering a new era. No longer viewed by the dominant political culture as a sustainable habitat, as a tool of navigation or even as an irrigation source for farmers, the rivers of the entire upper Columbia basin had become a commodity.

Residents of the areas slated for flooding still had not been directly consulted.

Reaction in the Arrow Lakes valley to the signing of the treaty was swift and unhappy. On January 20, a landowner named Christopher Spicer told Canadian Press that there was no such thing as compensation for his farmland, stating flatly: "I don't care if they want to give me half a million dollars." By early February, Arrow Lakes valley residents were beginning to organize their protest against High Arrow and the loss of productive farmland.[35]

---

[35] On February 9, the *Arrow Lakes News* reported that the Nakusp Chamber of Commerce was canvassing residents of the valley for funds to carry on "the High Arrow fight." A pamphlet, *High Arrow Is Paradise Lost*, claimed that "the final decision that will stop High Arrow rests now with the politicians in Ottawa and Victoria. Urgent representations

In early March 1961, the US Senate ratified the CRT by a vote of 99 to 1. Meanwhile, north of the border, the provincial government continued to favour the sale of downstream benefits to the Americans to finance the dams, while the federal government insisted that power should not be exported and downstream benefits should never be traded for cash. On August 1, 1961, the BC government announced a takeover of the privately owned BC Electric, providing an assured market for Peace River power.

***

I sit in the car, still shaking, as the wipers work furiously to clear the pelting rain from the windshield, fighting the impulse to reverse the car and race back across the boundary to my home. But I am being called to attention. I take a deep breath and cross the bridge across the Kootenay to the dam's interpretive centre. There I spend an hour reading artfully constructed panels about how wildlife are protected and fish habitats supported by the Army Corps of Engineers, as well as the predictable descriptions of the large amount of electricity generated by the dam and the implication that we could not live without it. Libby Dam's design paid more attention to fish issues. It is specially equipped to draw water from the deepest part of the reservoir, so that the coldest currents can cool the downstream tailrace and thus enhance summer fish habitat. In a river system dominated by migratory species such as sturgeon, bull

---

are needed now. Write your M.L.A., Randolph Harding, Parliament Buildings, Victoria: and your M.P., H.W. Herridge, c/o Parliament Buildings, Ottawa."

trout,[36] kokanee and Gerrard rainbow[37], however, water temperature is only one factor. Dams interrupt free access to habitat and nutrient transfer. The loss of both have been devastating factors in fish decline.

The summer rainstorm has eased by the time I head north again. Patterns of emerging sunlight glisten against the asphalt. The year the CRT was signed turned out to be another big water year. In 1961, heavy snows accumulated in the upper basin that winter. During the melt, the Kootenay rose high enough that a highway sign from Warland, Montana, was loosened from its perch. The sign floated downstream through the state's canyons, crossed into Idaho and over Kootenai Falls, and then made a U-turn into Canada again. From there, the wayward sign travelled north on Kootenay Lake currents until it reached the lake's West Arm. It bobbed a little further before coming to rest on a beach at the end of a 300-mile journey.[38]

---

[36] The upper Columbia's bull trout (*Salvelinus confluentus*) was for many years considered the same as the Dolly Varden (*Salvelinus malma)* but was reclassified as a separate species in 1980. There remains some local controversy because the species are nearly identical and can only be distinguished through genetic analysis. The naming and classification of the bull trout is further complicated by two facts: the common name Dolly Varden was used for *Salvelinus confluentus* in California as far back as 1870, according to Valerie Masson Gomez, whose grandmother operated a fishing resort on the Sacramento River dating from that time; and, *Salvelinus malma* does exist in BC, though *not* in the upper Columbia region. (Wikipedia, "bull trout.") If all this information confuses the reader, welcome to the club.

[37] The Gerrard is a unique rainbow trout particular to this upper Columbia region, typically weighing up to 20 pounds or more.

[38] That year, Columbia River flows at Birchbank, BC, near the

I feel somewhat like the Warland sign, although in this post-treaty world, I float now on a river of asphalt. Such a freewheeling road sign would not make it far today. I stop at a roadside pullout and step out to take in a view of the majestic Koocanusa reservoir, streaked with silvery flashes from the sun, framed in the distance by the commanding spires of the Rocky Mountains. This reservoir has its own pain, having displaced people and flooded communities. The Warland sign once travelled through a fluid river system that connected disparate worlds. It bobbed and swelled as part of the water's annual moving cycle. Like the fish and the river nutrients of old, it linked the various habitats of the upper basin.

The road south to Libby has been a long one. The road back – through the historical twists and turns of great ecological and human cultural loss – may well be even longer. The forks of lightning are a piercing reminder that the power of water cannot be dismissed easily. Nor do best-laid plans necessarily unfold as desired.

---

international boundary, surpassed the surging flows of the great flood of 1948. Flood impacts were restricted to a few Canadian riverside communities, including Trail. When the high water receded, the sign came to rest at Five Mile Creek, near Troup Junction, on Kootenay Lake's West Arm.

2. Silence, Exclusion and Controversy

Standing in the terminal for the harbour-to-harbour flight from Vancouver to Victoria, I exhibit too much excitement to be a regular. I have never been on a seaplane. Every seat in the tiny aircraft will be occupied. I have novice luck and assume the bird's-eye view in the seat beside the pilot. A light spring rain is falling as we take off over the muted estuary of BC's other great river, the Fraser. I can see the markers of ocean current swirling to meet the heavily silted river outwash. The fresh water and ocean participate in a tidal dance of great beauty that captivates me as the plane rumbles across the sky. During the decade of treaty negotiations, General McNaughton proposed blasting a tunnel between the Columbia River and Fraser drainages. This would have allowed water captured by the big dams he envisioned in the Rocky Mountain Trench to cycle downstream as far as Revelstoke, BC, then flow through to the Fraser, where more dams would create more power as the Fraser flowed west to the sea. The outcry against the idea was swift, largely because the plan could wipe out the commercial salmon fishery on the Fraser, but also because of the technical engineering challenges. The outcry to protect salmon seems ironic, given that Grand Coulee Dam had only a few decades earlier destroyed BC's other major salmon fishery. But the fishery on the upper Columbia was not a commercial one. It was a rich spawning ecosystem for salmon that fed another commercial fishery on the lower Columbia. Governments had not yet made the connection between healthy spawning grounds and healthy fish runs.

The float plane seems very small against McNaughton's big ideas. It's a quick flight to Victoria's tidy harbour surrounded by hotels and government buildings that service the provincial capital. I have come for a singular purpose: to read the transcripts from the 1961 Water License Hearings, conducted by the BC government for the three treaty projects in Canada: Mica, Duncan and High Arrow. Three hearings were held, and 450 objectors spoke. The dams had already been confirmed in an international treaty, so the consultation was not really consultation. But the transcripts record the voices of people who lived in the region, people who, for economic and emotional reasons, felt deep attachment to the valleys slated for flooding. The hearings were led by the water comptroller for BC, A.F. Paget. Paget ruled early on in the process that any specific discussions of the merits of the CRT would be "out of order," because the treaty was a signed, approved deal. This ruling essentially strangled any chance that public input might result in any real changes to the treaty that might consider the local situation. Everything had already been decided outside of the public eye, in the private corridors of political power.

The transcripts arrive at my reading table in a large, acid-free cardboard box. They run over 1,000 pages. I step into the river of words and the undertow of regret and raw emotion pulls me down. I had expected it. What I had not expected was another discovery: the government even overlooked consulting with its friend, local private industry.[1]

* * *

Revelstoke Civic Centre, Sept. 18, 1961, for Mica Dam:

Cominco registers concern about the impact of Columbia River water releases on their operation of Waneta Dam, just above the international boundary. They are particularly concerned about American projects on the Pend-d'Oreille upstream of Waneta that will be added into the system after the treaty dams have been constructed. Cominco points out the interdependence of the various tributary and main stem projects that are either functioning at the time or will be added by the treaty. They advocate careful development that considers all the local impacts.

Celgar Limited objects to Mica Dam because of damage to the logging company's ability to move log bundles along the Columbia waterway, from the thick forests above the proposed location of Mica to its mill downstream in Castlegar.

Robert C. Hume speaks both for himself and for the Revelstoke Rod and Gun Club, asking for repair of inevitable damage to spawning grounds and a comprehensive study of wildlife and fish ecology before flooding.

---

[1] Water License Hearings conducted by A.F. Paget, BC Archives, GR0880, Box 16.

*** *

Kaslo Drill Hall, September 21, 1961, for Duncan Dam:

Dick Neufeld, a long time trapper in the Duncan River valley, points to a map on the wall that details the area slated to be flooded over by Duncan Dam: "This is ... our feeding grounds in the winter for the game. The lakes aren't marked on here, but all this island here, there is a little slough where the geese hang out."

Richard Welton, representing the West Kootenay Rod and Gun Club Association, describes further ecosystem impacts from Duncan dam: "The flow of the [nutrients from the] Duncan River into Kootenay Lake can be traced as far south as Kaslo and at times even to Ainsworth.... 4,500 acres of waterfowl habitat – all to be inundated. The loss here cannot be over-emphasized."

The water comptroller, Mr. Paget, interjects: "Well Mr. Welton, wouldn't it be better for everybody concerned if we moved all the people out of BC and then you wouldn't have these problems?"

Michael Stewart, representing Kootenay Forest Products (KFP), in Nelson, BC, speaks of the sustainable forestry losses in the Duncan valley if it is converted into a storage reservoir: 1.1–1.9 billion board feet (2.6–4.5 million cubic metres) of saw logs and the same amount of pulp wood, and 86,000 acres of harvestable forest, with the potential for 19.6–27.6 million board feet (46,000–65,000 cubic metres) to be removed annually, in perpetuity.

*** *

Revelstoke, Nakusp and Castlegar, BC, September 26–October 4, 1961, for High Arrow Dam:

At these meetings, the government hears of more regional losses from industry and agriculture:

Celgar, which has a pulp mill in Castlegar, objects again, this time to the Arrow Dam, which will be located between its mill and the extensive forest-licence lands in the Arrow Lakes valley.

Mrs. Wallace Hall, a third-generation farmer with 279 acres of beef cattle and mixed grains in Sidmouth, voices concern about her limited options for moving her farming operations: "Where we are is extremely fertile, and when we look at lands in the Okanagan Valley, their land is not nearly as good as ours, and yet the value is much higher."

Robert C. Hume of the Revelstoke Rod and Gun club, speaking at his second of the meetings, calls it "a shocking thing" that no consideration has been given to fish and wildlife issues.

Anglican reverend V.B.H. Pellegrin (Nakusp): "The rights of the individual are left sometimes virtually unprotected."

Lottie Meyer Morton (360-acre farm at Slewiskin Creek with 2700 metres [9,000 feet] of waterfront): "If the High Arrow Dam is built, may I humbly suggest trucking out our good soil? I brought a specimen here ... which I am going to give to any soil lover."

Christopher Spicer (vegetable and dairy farmer, Arrow Lakes Farmers' Institute, Nakusp): The best soils "naturally lie on the valley bottom, the floor of the valley.... it will be impossible to operate the higher marginal lands economically."

Jean Waterfield Spicer, married to Christopher: "It is a sad thing that love of money should be put before love of country.... I realize that this objection of mine is a very small thing when viewed against the vastness of Columbia development, but when you add it to the feelings of many farm women up and down the lake who feel the same way, it should carry a little weight.... Are not we, the main sufferers from High Arrow, entitled to get a major slice of the pie, or have not my first suspicions been confirmed and there is no pie at all?"

Donald Waterfield: "Now I don't quarrel with Mr. Williston, certainly not with you [Paget], it is not your fault. It may not be Mr. Williston's even. But somebody has crossed us up."

C.S. Fowler (Trail): "If a spokesman for the B.C. Power Commission [Dr. Hugh Keenleyside] assumes that the people of Trail would wish to see 2,000 persons on the [Arrow] Lakes displaced to give *them* flood protection then he is sadly misjudging the people of Trail."

***

In the end, the comptroller did as instructed by the government and granted the water licences to build the dams, although he attached a few conditions:

1. BC Hydro must install fish-spawning channels at the Duncan and Arrow;
2. BC Hydro must create waterfowl mitigation at Duck Lake near Creston;
3. BC Hydro must construct a navigation lock at Arrow Dam to allow transport of log booms to Celgar's pulp mill;
4. the foreshore clearing of the High Arrow, Duncan and Mica reservoirs must be thorough and complete.

The comptroller offered no mitigation for losses of agricultural land, forestry resources or individual livelihood. The forest licences would be cancelled and the farmland in valley bottoms purchased by BC Hydro. Those living in the affected valleys would have to either leave the region, or find places to live on higher ground. The few mitigation projects he attached to the various water licences came only after strenuous objections. Those making the objections had to endure occasional sarcasm and constant impatience on the part of government officials.

Lottie Morton had carried her soil samples, packed in several old aspirin bottles, to the hearing in Nakusp. She labelled each of them with specific reference to her productive fields, enriched over millennia by the deposits from Columbia River flood cycles. The transcripts are a firm reminder both of the lack of consultation with people who would be affected and of the disconnect that often exists between national and local experience. Paget's sarcastic response to Richard Welton's request – that perhaps all the people of BC should be moved out to protect the region's wildlife interests – demonstrates an inability of the government treaty and its framework to respond to the nuances of a natural system inhabited by real people, people who were deeply attached to the place where they lived. The water licence hearings offered no opportunity for local people to provide a voice of influence. The treaty's formation and execution had left no room for anyone in a position of power and authority to listen. There was no time for truly listening to people who lived in the valleys slated for flooding. No time for patience, either, especially now that a treaty had been signed, sealed and delivered.

3. Standoff

Despite the speed and efficiency of the provincial water licence process, several local, national and international political factors chewed at the edges of the CRT as 1961 turned into 1962. Formal ratification of the treaty by Canada was still far from assured. Factors influencing the delay included the still-unresolved conflict between BC and the Canadian federal government over financing the projects. Recent changes in American policy had increased the feasibility of more storage dams being constructed in the US. In Canada, an energetic national campaign against the CRT undertaken by IJC chair General McNaughton was gaining traction. Residents of the Arrow Lakes valley began to organize and voice their strenuous opposition to High Arrow dam.

Perhaps the largest blockade to successful execution of the treaty was the standoff about how to finance the project. A year after the signing of the CRT, Premier Bennett remained insistent in his position: if no settlement on the financing of the Columbia could be found that was advantageous to BC, the Columbia would not be developed.[2] Ottawa continued to reject Bennett's proposal to use Peace River power for BC domestic and industrial needs and sell the downstream power benefits from the Columbia to the Americans in a lump sum. Bennett pressed on with his own agenda. In mid-March, the BC Legislature introduced the BC Hydro Act to amalgamate the BC Power Commission with BC Electric. The merged entities would form a large crown corporation under the name of the BC Hydro and Power Authority. In response to opposition and criticism over his single-minded pursuit of his vision, Bennett offered nine words: "We don't wilt. We don't quit. We don't scare."[3] On March 30, the BC Hydro Act passed.

On April 10, 1962, the US announced a proposal to construct Knowles Dam in Montana, part of a relaxation of US federal policy on financing storage facilities. Pressure was building on Canada to resolve its dispute with the provincial government or risk losing the valuable "first added" status that gave such favorable economic weight to the three treaty dams. A few weeks later, Canada's prime minister, John Diefenbaker, called a federal election. The opposition party leader, Lester Pearson, indicated a desire to renegotiate the treaty with the US and begin construction of the dams within 12 months. "Too much time has been lost in futile quarrels," Pearson declared. "We will get moving with the speed that would match the importance of this project."[4] On June 18, John Diefenbaker

---

[2] Swainson, 235.

[3] *Calgary Herald*, March 23, 1962.

[4] Victoria *Times Colonist*, April 7, 1962.

was re-elected, but this time with only a minority government that reduced his former mandate.

The provincial and federal governments remained at a stalemate over the financing of the CRT projects.

Just before the general election, General McNaughton was (he claimed) "removed" as co-chair of the IJC by Prime Minister Diefenbaker, whom he referred to as a "dictator."[5] These were fighting words, and the general would not go down without one. His resistance to the Treaty Plan grew more vocal and brazen. Issuing press releases and writing journal articles and pamphlets, he advocated forcefully for an "all-Canadian" development of the Columbia. This he promoted as the McNaughton Plan, asserting that the large downstream benefits calculated from High Arrow reservoir could not be justified by the loss of Canadian water sovereignty. In response, the lead Canadian negotiator for Canada, minister of justice Davie Fulton, defended the CRT and its design as best for Canada.

The quarrelling continued.

---

[5] Swainson, 227, notes 30–31.

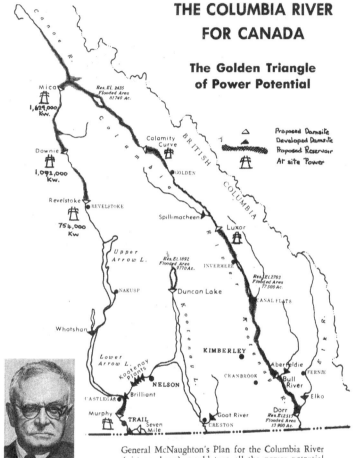

General McNaughton's Plan for the Columbia River (picture above) would turn all the power potential into actual Canadian Produced Electricity. *No Other Plan Will*. Half a Million New Jobs depend upon Adoption of the McNaughton Plan!

A. G. L. McNaughton.

During the Canadian political controversy over the CRT, and after his removal as chair of the IJC, General McNaughton produced a pamphlet, "Taming the Columbia," to communicate his ideas for Columbia River development to the general public. TOUCHSTONES NELSON MUSEUM OF ART AND HISTORY.

Everything Has a Price,
Even Betrayal

1. Growing Delicious Carrots

I am on the road again to Nakusp, a rural community located in the heart of the Arrow Lakes valley. There are no straight roads into the centre of the valley, only densely twisting and turning highways that navigate splendid and inspiring mountains, drop down into the valleys of various watersheds, and climb more mountain passes. Prior to the dams, people most easily accessed Nakusp by water, on a ferry system that ran north and south along the valley of the Columbia River and the Arrow Lakes from 1898 to 1954. Like the Sinixt people before them, those living in the valley enclosed by mountains had found water transport to be the most efficient. This ferry made many calls to small agricultural communities producing dairy, vegetables or fruit. Linked to a rail line and run by the Canadian Pacific Railway company, the system had worked well for half a century.

The same year that Kaiser Aluminum and the BC government announced the first (unsuccessful) proposal to dam the Arrow Lakes valley, Canadian Pacific Railway applied (successfully) to the BC government to cancel the ferry service. A newly privatized ferry system ran for a few more years, but it was clear even before the CRT had been signed that things in the valley were changing, largely in response to policies of the provincial government, which increasingly believed that the best and first value of the Arrow Lakes valley was as water storage.

Reading political and engineering accounts of the CRT and its formation, anyone can lose sight of the widening vein of pain in the local human experience. Agricultural settlement in the Arrow Lakes valley dated back only to about 1900, yet those residents who had succeeded in creating homes had found a piece of heaven that they would not relinquish easily. All of the people who spoke out ardently at water licence hearings against the flooding of the Arrow and Duncan valleys are dead now. The transcripts preserve a vivid, lively and at times emotionally desperate cry from the place itself. The plans to flood the valley permanently were that much more mystifying for residents because the BC government continued to promote the Arrow Lakes valley as a prime area for agriculture up to a few years before the treaty was signed.[1]

Among the most passionate advocates for preserving the agricultural life of the valley was Christopher Spicer. Spicer purchased his farm just after the Second World War, following service in the British Royal Air Force and then a worldwide search for good land where he could create the farm of his dreams. Well educated, articulate

---

[1] Waterfield, *Continental Waterboy.*

and focused, he fought hard against the eventual expropriation of his land. In the end, he was the only landholder in the valley to keep his name on title. To this day, his family owns and operates the small portion of the original farm that remains above the reservoir shoreline.

I've arranged to meet one of Spicer's twin daughters, a teenager at the time of the flooding. I want to hear from her exactly how it felt to lose a farm.

***

The same spring that McNaughton launched his offensive against the CRT, Richard Deane, an engineer working and living in the upper Columbia basin, awakened like a bear from hibernation when he realized that the Arrow Lakes valley would be destroyed by High Arrow reservoir. Deane was a local boy, raised on the east shore of Kootenay Lake by early 20th-century British immigrants. His first job was for Cominco in Trail, where he worked as a humble smoke-tester during the lean Depression years, sampling emissions from the smelting operation.[2] Over the years, he built a solid career

---

[2] As the 1920s drew to a close, the skies above the Columbia River were so dense with sulphur dioxide smoke (a by-product of smelting) that vegetation had burned away from the surrounding mountains almost as if a fire had swept through. The sulphur dioxide drifted south on the prevailing winds. When farmers in Washington State protested about the effects the acid rain was having on their crops, international arbitration through the IJC resulted in an order to curb emissions. The company soon began to convert the sulphur dioxide into agricultural fertilizer with the help of electricity generated at yet another power plant, constructed in 1932 on the Kootenay River at Corra Linn Falls. (Mouat.)

with Cominco, eventually overseeing its several run-of-the-river dams on the lower Kootenay River. A captain of industry, Deane believed that dams would always play an important role in the region's economic prosperity. Yet the construction of High Arrow Dam made little sense to him as both an engineer and a resident of the region. He asked for and received permission from his employer to study the project and add his professional opinions to the debate.

For the remainder of that year, Deane wrote letters to BC's water comptroller, then to federal bureaucrats, politicians and major daily papers, asserting that the High Arrow dam could "forever destroy the natural resources" of the valley.[3] When he specifically criticized the location and design of the dam, he was reprimanded by his professional association for having publicly spoken out against the work of fellow engineers.[4]

---

[3] To A.F. Paget, comptroller of water rights, Deane proposed an alternative to High Arrow discussed and favoured by McNaughton: a Low Arrow Dam at Murphy Creek just upstream of Trail, BC, with a maximum reservoir level in the Arrow Lakes valley of 427 metres (1,400 feet), more or less equivalent to the natural spring high water mark. In his letter, Deane calls the potential relocation of hundreds of people from the Arrow Lakes valley "an undesirable feature" of the plan specified under the CRT. (Richard Deane to A.F. Paget, March 2, 1962; personal papers of Richard Deane.)

[4] H.W. Herridge, the MP for Kootenay West, appeared to echo Deane's observations in Parliament, claiming that it was "the result of political rather than co-operative and effective planning." Suggesting that the federal government signed the treaty even before they knew the feasibility of the High Arrow Dam, he said that engineers "have gone down hundreds of feet" drilling at the dam site "and have not been able to find [bed]rock." Herridge reminded the House that the treaty had also been signed without any assessment of damage to 18 communities in the upper Columbia basin. (*Leader-Post,* December 14, 1962.)

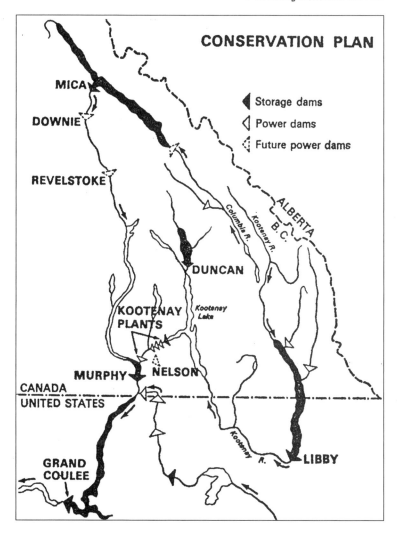

CONSERVATION PLAN

◀ Storage dams
◁ Power dams
◁ Future power dams

MICA

DOWNIE

REVELSTOKE

Columbia R.

Kootenay R.

ALBERTA
B.C.

DUNCAN

KOOTENAY
PLANTS

Kootenay
Lake

MURPHY   NELSON

CANADA
UNITED STATES

GRAND
COULEE

Kootenay R.

LIBBY

Richard Deane's alternative to the Columbia River Treaty plan did not include the High Arrow/Keenleyside project. FROM WATERFIELD, *CONTINENTAL WATERBOY.*

Undeterred, Deane shifted his efforts from criticism to advocacy for a new CRT, one that would be "Simple, Flexible and Open Ended." A self-described "long time resident of the area with conservation interests,"[5] Deane believed that the international water treaty should set out broad principles only. Specific projects, he felt, should be studied and discussed until there was universal agreement about where, when and how to build. When that idea met with government resistance, he next developed what he called the Conservation Plan and began to promote it actively. This alternative to the McNaughton and Treaty plans achieved the storage needed for hydro-power efficiency and flood control, destroyed the least land in both the East and West Kootenay valleys, and displaced the least number of people. "Surely," Deane said, "it is the duty of the federal government to preserve the land of Canada for Canadians."[6]

**

When I arrive at the Spicer farm buildings on a hot July day, there is no sign of Christopher Spicer's daughter Janet in the barns or in the old farmhouse, both of which are perched just above the Arrow reservoir's high water mark, where I duck behind compact rows of green beans, squash and leeks and change into my swimsuit. I squelch into the silt and muck laced with grass and weed. As I lose hold of the bottom and stroke out, I realize that I am swimming over Christopher Spicer's farm fields. Images of a stray carrot top, a ruffled rhubarb leaf and a shaft of asparagus float to the surface of

---

[5] "Talk to be presented to the I.E.E., Vancouver Section, April 1st, 1963." Richard Deane personal papers; courtesy of the Deane family.

[6] Quoted in Waterfield, *Continental Waterboy*.

my mind. The water feels haunted by a man's broken dreams. I turn
and slosh quickly back out.

I'm drying off when Janet drives into the farmyard and steps from
her car. She has the tall, regal bearing I have seen in photos of both
of her parents. Her eyes are large and intelligent, her hands permanently marked by years of work in the soil. She speaks breathlessly
of a need to prepare some vegetables for delivery to the local grocery store. I follow her into a cool, dark barn, its silos tilted with age,
its bright red paint faded to pale rose.

Today, the Spicer farm receives orders for 20 tons of carrots each
year – from private households, food co-ops and grocery stores in
the region. The carrots are a regional legend widely praised for their
sweet, crisp flavor. Janet sells every organic carrot that she plants.
She tells me she would grow and sell more if she could. It's no wonder, given the way they gleam from being carefully tended and
washed. The best of the family's fields are permanently under 12 feet
of water. The farmland that remains above the reservoir is far from
unaffected. The original Spicer farm is today bisected by a highway
constructed just above the new reservoir in the 1960s, and by a BC
Hydro power substation, both government-enforced easements.

In order to maintain official farm status on the 29 acres of marginal soil that remain above the high water mark of the Arrow
Lakes reservoir, Janet Spicer must work extremely hard. She culti-
vates her largest crops on other land that she has pieced together
through purchase or lease. Today, only a quarter-acre vestige of the
original field remains, tucked in between the high water mark of
the reservoir and the old farmhouse. Here, Janet grows vegetables
in some of the soil that Spicer's nephew transported up the hill by
backhoe in 1967, just before the reservoir water rose to cover the

fields. For at least two decades after the flooding, her father moved like a refugee from one-acre plot to one-acre plot as he leased and borrowed the land he needed to continue to grow produce. Janet describes the impact of the early years after flooding:

A successful farm is about continuity. The first year of ownership, a farmer might install fences. The next year, drainage. The year after that, a new barn. The investment grows over time. The CRT took away the control my father had assumed over our prosperity. We were, in a sense, homeless farmers.

Over the years, Janet's father assembled a patchwork of land that attempts to replace the compact ten acres in the original deed. After moving back home in the 1980s, Janet began to help. At Twin Lakes, for example, a ten-minute drive southeast of the farm, Janet grows the carrots as well as spinach on two acres of peaty loam, on a lifetime covenant of use granted by a friend. Tucked into a forest of cedar and hemlock, the micro-climate has only one frost-free month each year, far fewer days than the valley's average of 150. The crops she sows there don't mind the cooler weather. Rinsing spinach leaves, she emphasizes the positive.

The forest around the field protects it from carrot rust fly. The soil is lovely and soft. I seed them closely. The carrots like it. They squeeze that soft soil as they grow. Neither carrots nor spinach are much deterred by the light frost. We've made it work.

She twist-ties leaves into green posies and moves on to parsley.

Dad used to say that McNaughton was Canada's finest citizen. It was Bennett who spoiled everything. McNaughton had integrity. He wasn't afraid to stand up to the various governments and tell them they were making a decision that wasn't in Canada's best interest.

Her hands fly through the work. Mine scribble notes and turn pages.

***

As debate over the merits of the CRT Plan increased in the press, the provincial and federal governments continued to spar over how to finance the dams. Ottawa was holding firm on a policy against exporting power (or converting its monetary equivalent into downstream benefits). Bennett responded by saying that for BC, developing the Columbia was optional, with the Peace project taking first place in the provincial priorities. The US was growing more anxious for a resolution as the clock ticked closer to two years elapsed since ratification by the US Senate.

Near the end of 1962, government technical advisors conducted a re-examination of the costs of constructing High Arrow.[7] Through the autumn, as Bennett kept his feet planted in his position, pressure had been mounting on Prime Minister Diefenbaker from within his own government to resolve the issue of financing the CRT dams though advanced sale of downstream benefits. In December, representatives from the US and Canada gathered to negotiate a price for the power, should it be sold. Some Americans attending that meeting claimed that changes in the US system since 1960 meant that they could abandon the treaty without economic loss.[8] The CRT ship was being tossed up onto a very rocky shoreline.

In early January 1963, Diefenbaker took a stand against an American proposal to position nuclear weapons on Canadian soil, even

---

[7] Swainson, 237ff.

[8] Kennedy's administration was more inclined to grant federal funds to support dam construction than Eisenhower's had been. This relaxation of funding supported the development of Dworshak Dam (Clearwater River), the Boundary (Pend-d'Oreille) and Libby, among other American projects being considered south of the line.

after being urged by the NATO supreme commander to accept it. A month of political struggle followed, with Diefenbaker's Conservative minority government eventually defeated through a non-confidence vote. This triggered another federal election – the second in a year. Watching the political tumult from south of the border, US secretary of the interior Stewart Udall described the fall of the Conservative government as "a blow, but not necessarily a fatal blow" for the Columbia River Treaty.[9] Another, unnamed US government official was less cheerful, offering that he had been pessimistic about the treaty's ratification even before a diplomatic conflict over nuclear weapons arose between the two countries. His statements implied that the completed agreement now seemed highly unlikely.[10]

During the spring election campaign, the Liberal opposition party's prominent members assailed the CRT,[11] focusing criticism on

---

[9] If a new agreement with a new government could be reached within "about six months," he said, the two-year-old treaty could still be implemented. "But the more structures that are completed on our side of the river," he said, likely referring to the proposed Knowles project, "the more we are put in the position ... [that] it will not be equitable to do so." *Spokane Daily Chronicle,* February 7, 1963.

[10] *Calgary Herald,* February 2, 1963.

[11] Jack Davis spoke against the fact that, under the treaty, the price of the downstream benefits were to be set only after ratification. He believed that Canada was receiving an inadequate amount of money for flood control and pointed out that Canadian dams had a deadline while Libby Dam did not. In an address to the Portland Chamber of Commerce in mid-March, he urged renegotiation, though he clarified that this should be "in the matter of principles only." (Spokane *Spokesman-Review*, March 19, 1963.) Not long afterward, General McNaughton addressed the Association of Professional Engineers of

an inadequate payment for open-ended flood control and on what was seen as US control of water – both the Columbia River water to be stored in Canada and the Kootenay River water that would cycle through Libby Dam. Both the provincial and federal Canadian governments grew more defensive, with the federal government increasingly open to striking a deal with the Americans on a lump-sum sale of power. Such an agreement would appease Bennett and free up a portion of the downstream benefits to finance the dams. Whether or not this use of the benefits was true to the original intent of the treaty, it was at least a pragmatic response to the stalemate.

***

Janet carries on, describing how W.A.C. Bennett betrayed the citizens of the Arrow Lakes valley and deftly manipulated treaty negotiations in order to get the maximum cash he could get through the sale of downstream benefits. Bennett, she explains, had in 1960 played the High Arrow reservoir card through his BC negotiator, at one point switching his allegiance to a plan including Libby Dam

---

Alberta, openly criticizing the design of the treaty. McNaughton's words were much more contentious, observing that "the British Columbia government schemed to downgrade the advantages of the Columbia River project in order to put its Peace River hydro plans in a more favourable light." McNaughton claimed that US negotiators, with "very great assistance from the B.C. representative," were able to obtain clauses in the treaty that gave the US "effective control" of water storage in Canada. (*Saskatoon Star-Phoenix,* March 25, 1963.) A month earlier, forestry minister Ray Williston had criticized McNaughton directly in his annual address to the provincial legislature, describing him has "a man who has made his mark, is now past his prime, never has been an acknowledged hydraulic engineer, and now stands alone." (Quoted in Swainson, 247.)

because he knew the Americans wanted it, in order to get what he wanted – more money in the short term to construct the dams.

It wasn't just the act of being dispossessed, being stripped of every-thing we loved, being forced to watch it all being torn apart with chainsaws and bulldozers, set on fire or submerged, knowing that our wildlife was drowning, knowing that our river was dying along with all the natural life it had supported since the beginning of time, the kind of sadness associated with permanent loss; it was as much the conspiracy, the denial of democracy, being victims of a decision from which we were excluded. And then the betrayal by Bennett. Any-one resisting the project was wasting their time protesting it. It was a done deal from the day they signed the treaty, and the way things went after that just made it worse.

I stand beside the washing table, recording as fast as my pen can move. Today, those who have lived the betrayal directly are dwindling in number; many have died or moved on. While I am taken aback by the implications of her words, I know that media reports and the historical record accurately reflect a polarizing style, one Bennett employed to fulfill his own vision. Janet continues, displaying an extensive, almost encyclopedic knowledge of the cultural history surrounding the CRT.

The Columbia River Treaty was negotiated entirely in secret between 1950 and 1960 – long before the general public was made aware. No one in government cared about the people who lived here, who loved living here. No one here was consulted. My father suffered two heart attacks from the trauma of watching his land being flooded. In my view, he never fully recovered.

We were asked to sacrifice our way of life in the name of "progress." Why didn't anyone ask us what progress was?

***

Throughout the at-times acrid and partisan Canadian national debate about the merits and future of the CRT, Richard Deane's voice had risen as relatively impartial and apolitical. His Conservation Plan came right up the middle between the Treaty Plan and the McNaughton Plan, combining features from both. He asked political leaders to consider intangible values versus tangible dollar values. For Deane, the intangible values of people, justice, nationhood, water, beaches and recreational use such as fishing and boating needed consideration just as much as the tangible values: hydropower, kilowatt hours, economic prosperity, convenience, re-regulation and calculation of benefit-cost ratio. By reducing the amount of water stored from 15.5 to 12.5 million acre-feet, he said, the flood control expectations would still be met, though of course the up-front dollar value of downstream benefits would also be reduced.

Though he was well aware of and immersed in the national public debate, Deane was likely unaware of the government's realignment of costs for Arrow and the four highly confidential position papers prepared by technical staff in BC and Ottawa in the fall of 1962. A very real possibility was developing behind closed doors in government circles: Arrow might not be built at all. The Peace River power development was definitely going ahead. Bennett's tough stand against the federal government about financing the projects appeared to have worked, or even to have gone a little further than Bennett would have hoped. Ottawa's need to sharpen its pencils and test the financial viability of following through with the CRT commitment to build the dams had led to a broader discussion about the viability of the projects themselves. One position paper suggested renegotiating the treaty without the Arrow and Duncan projects. The costs of Arrow had sky-rocketed, in part because of the new water licence requirements to install a navigation lock for log transport and to clear the reservoir shoreline completely, both unforeseen when cost estimates had been developed, from 1957 to 1960. At the same time, technical staff also seriously questioned if there would be another chance to get the economic deal they had gotten in 1961, given the changes in US policy around federal support for water projects.[12]

The ratification of the treaty began to hinge on the Canadian federal government's long-held policy prohibiting international sale of electricity. That policy might have to be reversed in order to strike the deal with the Americans for downstream benefits. Other than renegotiation, the only way out appeared to be a deal that would maximize the up-front cash to pay for the projects, and the generous storage values apportioned to High Arrow in 1961 were one of the few remaining advantages.

***

Janet is still washing carrots. She explains that BC Hydro land agents initially offered her father $30,000 for his productive farmland. A strict "no negotiating" policy set by BC Hydro meant that refusal to accept an offer initiated an immediate legal conflict. Insulted by the low offer, Christopher Spicer did refuse, and hired a lawyer. During the legal process, BC Hydro sent a man named Swales, a leading horticulturalist from the Okanagan, to verify the

---

[12] For more on these reports, the politics surrounding them, and the policy rationale for the lump-sum sale of power, see Swainson, 237–42.

appraisal that justified their low offer. Swales instead determined that the Spicer farm was irreplaceable. He itemized the fertile soil, the irrigation from warm, subterranean springs, the moderate climate and the excellent sun exposure.

BC Hydro claimed that, as much as possible, they would offer replacement value. Janet describes how, between 1962 and 1964, her father drove 11,000 kilometres (7,000 miles) across British Columbia in search of a comparable farm that he could purchase. He found two possibilities: a 45-acre farm in the north Okanagan at Westwold, valued at $175,000, and a 20-acre farm in Duncan with rocky soil and a stone house for $125,000. Both dollar amounts were more than four times the "replacement" offer from BC Hydro.

Dad didn't really want a price for his land, though. He wanted his land. Those people with small holdings in the valley were expropriated first, for relatively generous settlements. Hydro held out against the larger land owners, people like my father, for whom replacement value would mean considerably more. Eventually, Hydro doubled their offer to Dad to $60,000. Beyond that price they would not budge. Dad needed $80,000 to be able to finance the purchase of either of the farms he had found. He wasn't a young man. If he was going to start over, he couldn't be in too deep a hole. Hydro continued to offer $60,000. That was their maximum. They stood firm. So did Dad.

Janet resumes the careful washing of her produce, her words flowing from the shoreline of nostalgia to that of bitterness and back again. She imparts what she knows breathlessly, as if there is never enough time. The rhubarb in her hands is deep pink, thick and glossy. As she sprays and scrubs with long, strong fingers, memories of the land as she once knew it pile up on each other with precise and articulate speed.

Here on the farm, Dad grew everything. Absolutely everything, from asparagus to zucchini. He used to say it took 1,000 years for a river to lay down one inch of topsoil. His soil was rich and deep, and he irrigated his fields from a thermal spring right on the property. It was a paradise. The shorelines and meadows were carpeted with blue camas, wild onions, Indian paintbrush, violets and bluebells. Most of the songbirds that used to populate the cottonwood forests in the natural flood plain are gone. The mergansers, bufflehead and goldeneye ducks can't survive without the small fishes to feed on. They're gone, too.

Only when she slows down does her voice tremble across a particularly difficult aspect of the flooding. Occasionally, the personal pain of her family's loss surfaces visibly on her face. Otherwise, she is dignified and composed as she reminisces about the family's numerous milk cows whose manure once fortified the soil in the vegetable fields, about a cottonwood forest on the property's northern boundary between the fields and the river, and about a wide verandah shaded by elm trees, where she slept every night that she could, sometimes right into winter.

Hanging on the wall behind her is a framed black-and-white photo of her father, taken after the treaty was ratified. Spicer leans against a Volkswagen van parked in the farmyard and wears a grim expression, a simple plaid shirt and work pants. Beside him, pounded into the ground, is a hand-painted sign: *High Arrow clears all property to this elevation 1460.* Near this photo is another one, of General Andrew McNaughton.

The "safe line" below which BC Hydro expropriated land for the reservoir ran right through the kitchen and living room of the Spicer farmhouse. Spicer knew that this line generously took into account susceptibility to sloughing or other impacts. He also knew

Christopher Spicer in his farmyard, circa 1962. COURTESY OF JANET AND CRYSTAL SPICER.

that the ground on which his house and barn rested was as firm as his love for the place. He sat at the kitchen table that hovered over the safe line and refused to budge.

Nearly 50 years later, Janet now focuses on maintaining farm status with the intensity of a woman seeking refuge from the trauma of loss. She persists with passion and integrity, growing organically, sometimes even from her own seed. She washes carrots until they gleam, and bundles greens as if they were flowers. She carries on.

You know, when landowners spoke passionately at the water licence hearings, the provincial water comptroller, Mr. Paget, ruled the testimony as "emotionally disturbed." When one resident asked him on what grounds he would deny the water licence to build the High Arrow, he replied that he would have to refrain from answering the question. He never had any intention of denying the water licence, of course. The hearings were a sham.

* * *

In April, 1963, Richard Deane spoke to the Vancouver chapter of the Institute of Electrical and Electronics Engineers. In his notes for the talk, Deane records his position on the CRT, arguing strenuously for its renegotiation: "A new Treaty should be Simple, Flexible and Open Ended, setting out principles only and allowing separate negotiations on individual projects.... Contentious projects such as High Arrow ... can be studied and discussed further until there is more universal agreement as to which should be built and when."[13]

To his professional association, Deane once again advocated for what he called "good" projects (Mica, Duncan, Libby and a

---

[13] "Talk to be presented to the I.E.E., Vancouver Section, April 1st, 1963." Richard Deane personal papers; courtesy of the Deane family.

Low Arrow dam at Murphy Creek) as opposed to those he called "questionable" projects for their cost, scope or destructive nature. (McNaughton's Bull-Luxor dam and High Arrow).[14] His arguments were rational and compelling but stood no real chance against an international treaty that had been designed by a team of international negotiators, signed, then delayed. Canada needed to make the best of what had become an awkward diplomatic situation. Renegotiation did not appear to be the answer, politically. Local concerns and values made little or no impact on the national stage as Canada grappled with rapid changes. Economic arguments held the most sway as a method for salvage.

On April 8, 1963, Lester Pearson led the Liberal party to victory over the Conservatives, forming a minority government. Residents of the Arrow Lakes valley had been hopeful over the past year that Pearson would renegotiate the treaty, as he had indicated during the campaign. But once elected, Pearson and his cabinet, perhaps influenced by the confidential position papers that had been quietly circulated to members of the Diefenbaker government in the fall of 1962, decided that a review of the CRT might jeopardize it altogether. By April 23, the Liberal leader and his new government had decided that potential gains from the review process did not offset potential losses.[15] Federal officials also announced that the government would soon secure an agreement with BC about the value of downstream benefits.

---

[14] Richard Deane to C.E. Marlatt, July 16, 1963. Richard Deane personal papers; courtesy of the Deane family.

[15] Swainson, 252.

In a letter to a colleague that spring, Deane considered his Conservation Plan "sort of lost cause, but I feel compelled to carry it through to conclusion for the land and the people involved."[16] That same day, he wrote another letter marked "personal" to another colleague in the BC Hydro gas department, saying, "I would not care too much for the dollars or kilowatts but for the land and the people I will travel this road to the end."[17]

***

Janet has finished washing and sorting vegetables for market and is leaning against the sink, her arms crossed, her face defiant. She explains how – from the date of the treaty's ratification, right through to the filling of the reservoir – her father made sure that someone was on the property constantly, out of fear that if it was left unoccupied, BC Hydro relocation officers might come to raze or burn down the buildings.

Do you know that Hydro budgeted only $20-million for all the land costs for people living in the valleys behind the three dams, Libby, Duncan and Arrow? They underestimated, of course. There wasn't enough money to buy people out generously; to make it worse, the dams were going over budget. The higher costs went, the less likely it was that people would be treated fairly. I think they got tired of fighting with us. Eventually, they paid Dad $60,000, returned the land titles that they had seized in the mid-'60s, and left him alone. He still had his farm buildings. And the quarter-acre of good soil

[16] Richard Deane to E.M. Stiles, May 1, 1963. Richard Deane personal papers; courtesy of the Deane family.

[17] Richard Deane, May 1, 1963. Richard Deane personal papers; courtesy of the Deane family.

above the high water mark of the reservoir. But really, how could there ever be adequate compensation for people who love where they lived?

Spicer was, like most farmers, a pragmatist. He encouraged his daughters to get summer work on the brushing crews that were clearing the reservoir. He also did plenty of clearing for hire. Janet describes her father's bitter reward for his vigilance and stubborn dignity: the right to stand at his kitchen window in the spring of 1969 and then again 1970, to watch as the coursing snowmelt met the resistance of the High Arrow Dam. Gradually, over two years, the reservoir filled, covering his farm fields with several feet of water. After the flooding, he never really took any pleasure in farming, though he did continue with the work where and how he could, on less fertile land above the high water mark. Without the energy and drive of his twin daughters, the enterprise of the Spicer farm might well have dwindled and disappeared as he aged, even if the farmhouse and barns remained standing.

After she has finished washing a pile of leafy greens, Janet straps a bucket to her waist and announces that it is time to pick green beans. I take the hint and make a move to leave. She says she has one more thing to say before I go.

After he died, I made an FOI [freedom of information] request for the documentation around Dad's dispute with Hydro. Boxes and boxes of documents arrived here one day. All those enormous stacks of paper, compared to the small shreds of paper that is his surviving land title. Today, it's the land title I value most, after all he went through. The title is undermined by a highway easement and a Hydro substation, and of course by the most significant easement - the one that allowed BC Hydro to flood the land in the first place. They can come onto this land anytime they like and do anything with it. But the Spicer name is still there, on the title record.

I say goodbye and drive to the top of the hill to look back at the reservoir – 7.1 million acre-feet of water, its use and the level of the reservoir governed largely by the CRT. It's early summer, and the annual snowmelt has expanded to fill the entire valley. The once beautiful, productive valley is now a smooth, unnatural plane of liquid lit by late-afternoon sun. In *Life Is a Miracle*, the American conservationist Wendell Berry says that "we know enough of our own history by now to be aware that people exploit what they have merely concluded to be of value, but they defend what they love." The force of change that created the CRT projects was too great, the international agenda too complicated, and the political personalities too forceful for the inhabitants of the Arrow Lakes valley to do much more than move reluctantly out of the way. I drive away into the mountains, wishing that the era of exploitation of land for any purpose could come to an end.

I have heard policy murmurings that those hoping to restore salmon in the upper Columbia system will seek an infusion of cold, clear water to charge the mid and lower Columbia River in the US. Some advocates say this could be achieved by keeping the Arrow reservoir at full pool throughout the year. Proponents of this approach need to open their ears to the history of the valley's losses and the deeply harmful effects of unnatural water storage. The valley, so wounded and nearly destroyed by industrial water development, sorely needs some of its land to be recovered, both as ecosystem and as human home.

The power of love has limits.

2. End Game

In mid-May 1963, after a two-day meeting with President Kennedy in Hyannis Port, Massachusetts, Prime Minister Pearson indicated that his government would ask only for "adjustments and clarifications" to the treaty – not a new agreement.[1] Pearson left a memo with Kennedy outlining five aspects of the treaty that had caused domestic criticism. Two were of particular concern: in the 1961 agreement, Canada had given up all of its right to divert the upper Kootenay River; it had also neglected to clarify the extent of Canadian responsibility for US flood control after the first 60 years of the treaty.[2]

---

[1] Spokane *Spokesman-Review,* July 11, 1963.

[2] The other three items were: a specific agreement that allowed downstream benefit sales to be lumped together for the first 30 years of the treaty only; a request for a waiver of stand-by transmission charges

On July 8, 1963, Canadian federal leaders finally signed an agreement with BC Premier Bennett to set the terms for how the dams would be financed: a lump-sum sale of downstream benefits for a fixed time. Under the terms of this accord, BC was to be sole agent for fulfilling treaty obligations with regard to dam construction. BC taxpayers would be responsible for cost overruns, and BC Hydro would assume responsibility for construction and relocation. Still to be worked out precisely was the issue over how much monetary value to give to the limited sale of downstream benefits, though the concept of attaching a protocol to the treaty concerning the sale seemed to be a near-certainty.[3]

All that remained was for the US and Canada to set a price for the 30-year purchase and to itemize the specific changes to the 1961 treaty that would smooth the way to Canadian ratification. In early August, just after formal talks with the US in Ottawa, Liberal finance minister Paul Martin flew west to Portland, Oregon, to meet with Charles Luce, head of the US Bonneville Power Administration. Media reports of his discussions with the American entity responsible for marketing Columbia River power hinted at the Canadian government's new focus on the lump-sum sale. On August 8, Martin told the *Ottawa Citizen* that "the price must be high enough from the Canadian point of view to make its share of the Columbia projects self-liquidating."[4] Bennett's vision had been

---

in the event of a sale; and a request for some degree of coordination where possible and without disadvantage to the US between operation of Libby and downstream Canadian plants. (Swainson, 409, note 4.)

[3] Swainson, 253–57.

[4] Statements such as this one contributed to a perception that the sole purpose of the downstream benefits was to finance the CRT projects,

realized. The fervent nationalism of McNaughton and his wish for Canada to receive downstream benefits annually in power only as a Canadian Entitlement had slipped downstream. For the time being.

Ratification of the treaty was within sight.

In spring of 1964, the government presented the CRT with its new protocols to the External Affairs Committee in the Canadian Parliament, distinguishing itself almost immediately from Diefenbaker's government in its circulation of a good deal of information that had been kept behind closed doors during negotiation and more than two years of controversy.[5] The hearings took place over six weeks and involved nearly 50 witnesses, including General McNaughton and Richard Deane.

Despite the new government's efforts to act with greater transparency, however, the committee hearings still exposed an uneven ground when it came to information. The technical staff had so entirely tested the cost-benefit legitimacy of the CRT during the two years of Canadian controversy that their argument for the CRT projects was nearly unassailable on economic terms. Those representing more values-based perspectives, such as water sovereignty or preservation of agricultural land, could not penetrate the tightly defended technical and strictly economic justification, much of which now hinged on the sale of the downstream benefits for a 30-year term. The hearings made obvious both the enormous complexity of the technical data and the great disadvantage of anyone testifying without significant technical support for their position.

---

rather than the benefits being established first as a principle of fairness, and only second, through political events, becoming an expedient and temporary form of financing for the dams.

[5] Swainson, 273–74.

Those who understood the finer engineering and economic points ended up controlling the debate and therefore appeared in possession of the best choice.[6]

The Columbia River Treaty was approved by Parliament on June 5 by a vote of 108 to 16, with less than half of its members present. The Senate also approved it easily on June 10. Less than half an hour later, the chair of BC Hydro signed the first major construction contract for Duncan Dam. The race to complete the projects was on.

---

[6] For more on this dynamic, see Swainson, 275–77.

The CRT Hangover

1. Speed, Efficiency and a Sideways Slip

The Columbia River Treaty detailed the specific storage dams, imposed deadlines and offered bonuses for early completion, to be paid by the Americans. These deadlines were motivated in large part by a pressing social concern in the US for flood control. In the political atmosphere of Canada's financial concern over the increased cost estimates, for Arrow in particular, these bonuses became an enticing motivator. On BC's fiscally conservative political stage, players were focused on the bottom line. The extra payments for early completion had a special gloss. And so it was that speed and efficiency framed the process, even if care and consideration for other values were sacrificed. All three Canadian CRT dams were completed in one decade. This remarkable engineering accomplishment generated considerable social and ecological chaos in its wake.

***

A map-lover interested in CRT history knows a gem when she sees one. I spread open a standard 1950s automobile-touring map of British Columbia to find and trace the Trans-Canada highway in eastern BC. Before the construction of Mica Dam, the highway wrapped around the Big Bend of the Columbia, passing right by the historic Boat Encampment, a major crossroads during the fur trade period. At the BC–Alberta border, the highway exits the Rocky Mountain divide through the Kicking Horse Pass and begins to follow the Columbia River as it flows north and downstream. I trace my finger as the highway follows the water from Golden past Kinbasket Lake and reaches the apex of the Rocky Mountain Trench, where three major mountain ranges converge and the Columbia hooks decisively south. From there, the road swings around the Big Bend in the Columbia to the confluence of the Wood and Canoe rivers. At this U-turn, a red dot marks Boat Encampment, not much more than a gas station and a store in the 1950s. Fur trade explorer David Thompson first gave the place this name after spending the winter of 1811 building a cedar clinker boat to take him south after the ice thawed, in the upstream direction, along the Columbia and toward the Kootenay in the Rocky Mountain Trench. Winter had stranded Thompson there after a successful but delayed attempt to find a safe and reliable way across the Rockies to the Columbia's main stem, since the Pikani people had blocked passage further south.[1] The area was also known and used by the Arrow Lakes

---

[1] In autumn 1810, Thompson had formed a party of men with the hope of breaching the Continental Divide between the east-flowing Whirlpool River and the west-flowing Wood River. His ambitious trip

Indians. Their name for it – *k'lsnxtl'ulhxtn* – means "at the ground-hog place," referring to the native species of marmot (*Marmota caligata* and *Marmota flaviventris*). Groundhogs thrive in high mountain environments, hibernating through long, cold winters and enjoying a varied diet of insects, bird eggs, plants and berries.

In his journals, Thompson described the area around Boat Encampment as a "wide alluvial, on which are forest Trees of enormous size." He made note of cedars up to 11 metres (36 feet) and pine up to 13 metres (42–43 feet) in circumference. Some trees, he remarked, grew 61 metres (200 feet) up without a branch. He was in a terrain of remarkable, old-growth coniferous forest. In his age of exploration, his measurements of these trees were not just idle admiration. The mapmaker likely had ship masts on his mind.

Today, Boat Encampment sits submerged beneath 183 metres (600 feet) of water, covered by a modern reservoir that traces its existence back to the very moment in history when Thompson first wintered there. Within the year, Thompson had departed from the upper Columbia region with enough measurements to chart the path of what he and others called the Great River of the West. He returned to Montreal, where he created his map with the real-time measurements he had taken using simple instruments and

---

across Athabasca Pass so late in the season, loaded with supplies for establishing the network of trading stations, proved to be one of his greatest challenges yet. When the party finally breached the west slope of the Rockies in early December 1810, they were met by unseasonable rain. The already deep snows had temporarily softened, making further progress nearly impossible. As the calendar turned to 1811, Thompson sent the most disagreeable men east back over the Divide, giving them the canoe emptied of supplies so that when they reached the Athabasca River again, they could float downriver. (Nisbet.)

assiduous mathematical calculations, made possible by hard slogging across the surface of the Earth. His measurements and the map he created were both accurate enough to serve colonial needs of the region for the next 50 years.

If our contemporary cultural attitude toward water in the Columbia River basin has a taproot, it reaches back to Thompson, one of the many Europeans who travelled the world for exploration, discovery, extraction and export. Born at a time when the ages of Reason and Romanticism overlapped, Thompson had basic scientific training, a colonizing curiosity, and a hunger to engage directly and somewhat innocently with wild nature.[2] The gradual development of natural sciences had led him and all the colonial officers like him to this point. One must map and catalogue the world before it can be conquered. One must strike a path through the wilderness before making commercial use of the raw resources in a landscape.

I set aside the road map and pull forward the Canadian government's 1956 survey maps. Thompson's "wide alluvial" is still there, fully 145 years later. This map records more specifically the variety and movement of the river's shoreline. Free-flowing water often hosts ecological complexity. In the world of a river basin, complexity is a synonym for a different sort of prosperity. On the survey map, the Columbia twists and winds through the Big Bend valley, its stream bed fringed by marshes, coniferous forests of cottonwood and birch, and areas labelled by the maps as "hay, grass or grazing land." Here – in these patches of wild meadow resembling

---

[2] Cultural historian Richard Holmes has observed that "the notion of an infinite, mysterious Nature, waiting to be discovered or seduced into revealing all her secrets" was widely held during the fur trade era.

those found in the high alpine – is the historical groundhog habitat that the Sinixt place name records. The 1956 maps focus on valley bottoms, with no information recorded above them. All around the edges of the surveyor's highest vertical measurements is a sea of white. The dense network of rapidly ascending mountains that cradle the northernmost path of the Columbia was not recorded here. I pick up my notebook and copy the line of the Big Bend Highway as it travelled like the river it follows, passing through the alluvial wilderness with tributary systems descending all around it from the Continental Divide, the water forming patterns like branches on a tall, thin tree. A familiar hunger rises in me. I know that Thompson's "wide alluvial" has been flooded out by a reservoir. What lies beneath the surface of the reservoir behind Mica Dam? I want to see for myself.

The search for Boat Encampment has begun.

***

Construction of the treaty dams started almost immediately after ratification. Before the structures could go up, they needed a firm foundation. Powder monkeys drilled and inserted dynamite charges, then lit the fuses. Earth-moving and grading followed. Duncan would be an earth-filled dam that traversed an ancient rock canyon. This canyon was already 365 metres (1,200 feet) deep, with sediment deposited by glaciers and the river. A third of it was an unstable mix of fine sand and gravel. Two leading soil mechanics – Dr. R.M. Hardy, dean of engineering at the University of Alberta, and R. Peterson of the Prairie Farm Rehabilitation Administration in Saskatoon, Saskatchewan – helped Montreal Engineering, the firm hired by the government, to design and construct the dam to allow for sediment to settle as much as 14 feet or more during construction.[3] Successfully meeting technical challenges was something BC Hydro and its contractors were to excel at during the construction phase.

What was to prove entirely more difficult to manage were the cultural, social and ecological complications that arose from construction. It was in this realm that the rapid execution of the projects created chaos and disappointment.

Crews completed Duncan Dam in April 1967, one year ahead of schedule, earning BC Hydro over C$4-million in a bonus under the terms of the treaty. The province took the bonus in the form of much-needed electricity from the US, rather than money. This added to the C$12-million flood control allocation already received for the project. With its early completion and without any workers killed or maimed,[4] the dam was in many respects an early success story. In 1969, Montreal Engineering won an award of merit from the Association of Consulting Engineers of Canada.[5]

Things appeared to be off to a fine start.

From the beginning, the High Arrow project provided more challenges, ones that grew more expensive and time-consuming to meet than those of Duncan. The half-concrete, half-earth-filled design, like Duncan's, was meant to accommodate the chosen site.[6] A rock outcrop stretched partway across the river, at which point the ancient channel dropped away, with the bedrock buried under silt about 150

---

[3] *Arrow Lakes News,* July 1969. (This source erroneously identifies Peterson's organization as the Prairie Farm Rehabilitation *Authority.*)

[4] Stanley.

[5] *Arrow Lakes News,* July 2, 1969.

[6] Long (488 metres/1,600 feet) and relatively low (52 metres/170 feet).

School children in 1965, watching blasting and construction for Duncan Dam. TOUCHSTONES NELSON MUSEUM OF ART AND HISTORY.

metres (500 feet) deep, deposited over thousands of years. Engineers mastered the challenge of strengthening the dam's footings by creating a sloping, impervious blanket of silt that spread from the dam 670 metres (2,200 feet). Put in place by special bottom-dumping barges, the 25-to-44-centimetre-thick (10-to-17-inch) blanket would limit seepage and reduce water pressure on the foundation.[7] Engineers calculated that the barges could release at least 190 cubic metres (250 cubic yards) of silt in about eight seconds and that the blanket would require a certain number of barge loads. Unfortunately, as the fill descended, it separated and dispersed, requiring twice as many loads as originally planned. According to BC Hydro, the blanket expertly addressed the engineering issues, but costs continued to mount as the river swallowed up load after load of silt. The navigation lock, a requirement from the water licence process, also presented significant construction challenges that increased the price tag on High Arrow.[8]

Producing three dams in ten years required a large army of workers, not all of whom could be highly skilled. The intense pace of construction around the province in the 1960s had created a high demand for labour, and consequently some green workers were hired for the Arrow project.[9] Widely promoted as an economic bonus for the region, dam construction created a strong, short surge of employment. Many workers received training in various

---

[7] IEA Hydropower Implementing Agreement Annex VIII – Environmental Mitigation Measures and Benefits Case Study 05-07: Water Quality – Arrow Lakes G.S., Canada. http://ieahydro.org.

[8] BC Hydro, *Columbia Construction Progress: Arrow Project – Review of Construction* (BC Hydro and Power Authority: Vancouver, July 1969).

[9] Stanley.

trades, though only a fraction of them could stay on in jobs that could support them once the projects were completed.

Mica's construction and design became both the physical and economic pinnacle of the three CRT projects in Canada. Slated to be the highest earth-filled dam in the entire world by the time it reached 240 metres (787 feet), the project's ambitious design had attracted the attention of engineers from around the world who wanted to be part of the technically challenging project.[10] Yet the remote location, long winters and unforeseen costs helped to pull the energy of execution sideways.

The region's resources and goodwill were increasingly strained by the rapid pace of construction of all three CRT projects.

***

The modern highway linking the community of Revelstoke to Mica Dam is smooth and well-groomed, despite the rugged and isolated surroundings. This 135-kilometre road exists and is maintained not for quirky dam tourists and researchers but for BC Hydro employees who service and upgrade one of the most profitable dams in the province. Mica produces a staggering 2805 megawatts of generating capacity, the highest in today's system of projects in southeastern BC.

I travel steadily north with my family in tow, having promised a weekend of camping and fishing at the reservoir. We cross a sturdy concrete highway bridge that spans the Goldstream River, a tributary of the Columbia. Aptly named, the river gushes milky-saffron with minerals washed down from the Selkirk Mountains high

---

[10] Ibid.

above. Today, I see no hint of the 2,000 gold-seekers who arrived after the fur trade in the 1850s and '60s. No sign of miners sluicing the rivers and streams, battling deep snows and avoiding floods. While a few who worked the Goldstream River got rich, most returned broke.[11] The gold rush in this remote corner of the Columbia River watershed was short-lived.

The highway to Mica Dam runs parallel to Lake Revelstoke reservoir, which contains the Columbia River water that has exited Mica's generators only to be held back again by Revelstoke Dam downstream.[12] Stained by silt from icefields hovering high above the valley, the glacial water in this slim run-of-the-river reservoir shifts from blue-green to cerulean and back to an almost surreal turquoise that takes my breath away. I stare out the window of the car as we hurtle along. The reservoir stares back at me, as pellucid as a striking pair of eyes.

***

Engineers had considered several designs for Mica, including the possibility of a poured concrete arch, similar to Grand Coulee, Shasta and Hoover dams in the United States. But the confluence of the Wood, Canoe and Columbia rivers contained such a rich source of glacial silt, sand and gravel that engineers decided it could be formed into a solid earth wall. During construction, the *Nelson Daily News* reported, "heavy construction equipment never before used in BC is being used to scoop millions of yards of material

---

[11] Leighton.

[12] Constructed in 1984 to regulate and make use of the outflow from Mica, Revelstoke Dam is now one of the most efficient and productive of the dams in the upper Columbia system.

from the riverbed to provide a rock bed for the dam."[13] By the time the dam was completed, dump trucks had transported 32 million cubic metres (42 million cubic yards) of fill from the river beds around Boat Encampment to build up the wall of the dam over several hundred feet from the valley floor. Specially built, 200-ton bottom-dumping trucks worked 20 hours a day from March to November for three years to transport the material from the river confluence to the dam.[14] The expanse of Boat Encampment, where Thompson had built his canoe in early 1811, was transformed into a "borrow area," the term for a source of sand, gravel or clean fill for a major construction project.

* * *

We have been in the car for over six hours. My school-aged sons are fractious. Their father, ever the competent driver, is ready to quit. I sold this trip to everyone as a camping weekend, but by early afternoon, that story has worn a little thin. At one point, the 13-year-old removes his earbuds and inquires sarcastically about where I am taking them now. I laugh, admitting that I'm not entirely sure myself. I encourage them to be grateful that I left them home for the trip to Grand Coulee. *We will be there soon.*

Finally, Mica Dam's massive, curving apron flashes into view, further up the ever-narrowing valley through which the Columbia flows. Even from a distance, the dam is impressively large, rising nearly 245 metres (800 feet) above the floor of the valley. If I hadn't read that it is earth-filled rather than concrete, I wouldn't believe

---

[13] June 22, 1968.

[14] Stanley.

it. I lose sight of it several times again as the car twists and turns north through the river channel. Finally, we climb away from the riverbed and draw closer to the dam itself. Just past the dam's crest, the asphalt road reverts to packed gravel. A large sign erected by BC Hydro plainly warns us of the hazards of boating on Kinbasket reservoir, citing weather and water levels that can change quickly. Another, much smaller, brown sign refers to a heritage marker up ahead. Though it makes no specific reference to David Thompson, I can sense that we are on the right track.

***

In the halcyon days of dam construction, BC Hydro suggested that the reservoirs and dams in the region would have a high tourism value, estimating that "hundreds of thousands" of tourists would pass through the region to admire them. In the 1960s, the mountain landscape around the confluence of the three rivers slated to be flooded by Mica Dam was referred to by planners as swampy and isolated, the rivers unnavigable and isolated. The dam and the flooding of the valley would, government officials claimed, make the area accessible and enjoyable and would "for the first time provide access to a vast wilderness area of spectacular beauty."[15] A *Nelson Daily News* article from the 1960s describes how the dam will "link the Selkirk and Monashee mountain ranges to form an 80-mile mountain-ringed lake" to "attract tourists."[16] The approximately 35,000 acres of land expected to be flooded was listed by BC Hydro

[15] "Mica: Key to the Columbia." BC Hydro promotional pamphlet, 1979–80.

[16] *Nelson Daily News,* June 22, 1968.

as having been "swamps, open areas and water surfaces."[17] Flooding the "swampland" into a recreational lake seemed like a good idea.

The land to be converted to reservoir behind Mica Dam was part of a vast wilderness area between the communities of Valemount and Golden. In 1941, the BC government had established this region as a 2.5-million-acre wilderness preserve: Hamber Park, as imposing in size as the Rocky Mountains that formed its eastern boundary. In 1961, taking into consideration the large tracts of commercial forest land and the pending Columbia River Treaty developments, the park's boundaries were radically redrawn. By the mid-sixties, it had shrunk to 55,600 acres, focused on the upper Wood River and the high alpine environment of Fortress Lake.[18] The entire area of the proposed Mica reservoir was at this point released from park boundaries.

* * *

When we pull in, the reservoir is calm and the sun is still hot. A boat is anchored just off shore, and I see a converted school bus parked at one campsite. Potlatch Creek Recreation Site sits very near the westernmost reach of Kinbasket reservoir's west arm, tucked in

---

[17] In the 1950s and '60s, "swamp" was a common synonym for wetlands and shallow water areas. From an agricultural perspective, these areas had limited use or value. In terms of ecosystem productivity, wetlands and shallow water areas provide fecund habitat for many aquatic and terrestrial species. At the time of the report, the ecological productivity and value of these areas was either less understood or minimized. See BC Environment & Lake Use Committee, *Mica Reservoir Region Resource Study*.

[18] "Master Plan for Hamber Provincial Park," December 11, 1986, Ministry of Environment and Parks file no. 2-3-3-80.

just a kilometre behind the dam crest. When workers then living in the Mica Creek village, several kilometres downstream of the dam, successfully petitioned BC Hydro for travel time, the corporation created this camp to eliminate travel costs. It appears that it was converted into a public recreation site after the completion of the dam.

Though it is a beautiful August weekend, all the other sites are vacant. As my sons burst from the car, I remind them that by canoe, the journey up the Arrow Lakes valley and beyond to Mica Dam commonly took 12 days or more and involved discomforts ranging from cold and wet feet to hunger and exhaustion. They don't seem to care.

We spend the next morning at the beach, a rather generous term for the expanse of fractured rock, heaped silt and scattered driftwood stumps that adjoin the water. Here in this unnatural shoreline is the exposed skeleton of what was once a forested slope, washed clean by the raising and lowering of water in the reservoir. Given Mica's role as a primary storage facility for the entire Columbia River power-generating system from source to sea, Kinbasket reservoir water levels can fluctuate dramatically, sometimes several vertical feet in just a few days. In August, just after filling, the reservoir tends to offer more consistent water levels. The air is already hot, the water a sheet of inviting blue-green glass. In the distant east, the Rocky Mountains rise from the watery horizon and echo their grandeur back onto the glassy surface. There is no sign of the campers from the school bus; it feels as if we are the only people in the world. The younger son fishes from shore and, without trying too hard, catches a two-pound whitefish.[19] I swim in water so clear

---

[19] Given the large number of nutrient-rich inflowing streams into

and clean that from a distance I can see the wood grain pattern on a tree stump submerged just off shore. I stroke out to it and crouch on the cut surface of the stump for a few minutes, warming my upper body in the sunshine before rushing back to shore through the icy-cold water.

Kinbasket Lake reservoir stores 20 MAF of water. It is hard to fathom the volume of 20 MAF, even standing beside it. Hydro-engineers call about 8 MAF of the 20 "dead storage." The position of the power generators in the dam makes anything below a certain depth unavailable for power production. The amount of "dead" storage at Mica equals the entire storage in Arrow Lake reservoir, which hints at the immensity of water stored in the submerged "wide alluvial" surrounding Boat Encampment.

In the afternoon, we drive east and south on the gravel road, on what begins as a fruitless search for the heritage marker. We are near the point of turning around when we see a retired fire warden driving toward us. He has been crawling around the remote back-country on a maze of logging roads, flushing out the odd camper he fears could become trapped by a lightning fire that started a few days earlier. He knows the Boat Encampment heritage marker well and points us back along the road we have just come down, to a cleared area where we can park. We retrace our path, park and spend another half hour searching for the head of the trail that he had said was obvious and would lead to the marker. Finally, by bushwhacking directly toward the reservoir shoreline in the

Kinbasket reservoir, its relatively remote location and consistently cold water, the reservoir's fishery for burbot, bull trout, kokanee and whitefish is healthier than the other reservoirs in the region. (Steve Arndt and Karen Bray, personal communication, February 10–11, 2011.)

general direction of the confluence, we stumble over a four-foot-high stone cairn that commemorates Thompson's boat-building winter and the fervent activities of a fur trade that opened the entire region for settlement by Europeans. Standing next to the cairn, I look out across the immense sheet of water. Commercial extraction has transformed the fur trade crossroads into a freshwater ocean, with nary a ship in sight.

***

At the opening ceremony for Duncan Dam on August 17, 1967, W.A.C. Bennett's pride was obvious as he declared that the dam had created a reservoir to be renamed Duncan Lake,[20] one that he predicted would soon be "a haven for pleasure boats, beaches for swimming, a place where, forever, we will find physical and mental benefits."[21] Bennett expressed a widespread belief that the narrow, densely wooded valleys – marked originally by rocky rivers, narrow, deep lakes and pockets of shallow water or wetland – were being transformed into something uniform, accessible and much more useful.

Bennett stood at the new viewing platform before a calm expanse of water covering a cleared reservoir, but just out of sight around the bend, reality beckoned. Two log booms had been positioned to capture the large amount of timber and brush that had either been felled hastily in advance of the dam's completion, or left standing. According to displaced residents from the nearby community of

---

[20] As well as flooding large areas of the Duncan River, the reservoir also absorbed Howser Lake. Its south end was formerly located a few kilometres upstream from the dam site.

[21] *Nelson Daily News.*

W.A.C. Bennett, premier of British Columbia, left, standing with unidentified men at the ribbon-cutting for Duncan Dam, spring 1967. PHOTO BY ART STEVENS. TOUCHSTONES NELSON MUSEUM OF ART AND HISTORY.

Howser, in the months leading up to the fill, BC Hydro had paid contractors $650 per acre to clear the area that would be in view at the opening ceremony. In the rush to do so, both marketable and unmarketable timber was logged and burned on the spot. What particularly irked residents was the fact that cleared land close to the dam near the mouth of Glacier Creek had been expropriated a few years earlier for only $50 per acre.[22]

Under the terms of the water licence, BC Hydro had five years after the completion of the dam to clear the Duncan reservoir, though in

---

[22] Larry Greenlaw, telephone interview by author, May 2011.

reality it was far longer before boats could skim across the water's surface. As the copious flow from the Duncan River watershed was held back that first spring, the valley gradually transformed into a chaotic mess. Several prospectors' cabins lifted from their foundations to ride the trapped current. Four-foot-thick chunks of marshland broke loose from the riparian. A great deal of marketable timber was waterlogged. The provincial media dubbed the reservoir "Bennett's Lake." The *Nelson Daily News* called it "a sportsman's and conservationist's nightmare." Conservation authorities touring the dam later that summer told the *Daily News* that "the lake is ruined for at least 50 years."[23]

Following the completion of Duncan, provincial resources minister Ray Williston justified the limited clearing of the reservoir to the Federation of BC Naturalists by claiming that the "best interests of the people of the province will be served by allowing natural forces to take out the trees."[24] Slowly, BC Hydro began the process of clearing the debris floating in the new reservoir, but they installed no boat ramps, graded no new beaches and did not establish any provincial parks in the Duncan valley. The debris-clearing work was not declared finished for 15 years.[25]

Due to the specific terms attached to the water licence, the controversy over Duncan would not be repeated at Arrow reservoir, where work crews felled mature cottonwoods, birch cedar, hemlock and orchard trees with chainsaws, and bulldozed willows more thoroughly, gathering them and other low-growing riparian vegetation

---

[23] *Nelson Daily News*, August 18, 1967.

[24] *Arrow Lakes News,* August 6, 1969.

[25] BC Hydro annual report, cited in Stanley.

into burn piles. Once lit, this green vegetation smoldered in giant piles for days on end. "In the fall of those years," valley resident Donald Waterfield recalled, "there was a pall of smoke blanketing the valley, adding materially to the depression of the people."[26] In preparing Arrow reservoir, BC Hydro also burned the buildings and other infrastructure that owners had not moved to higher ground at their own cost: barns, wharves, stores, churches and farmhouses. These burnings typically happened at night and sometimes without warning to neighbours, who often did not know if a fire was intentional or accidental. Burton resident Helen Buerge recalled the "horrible smell that used to hang about the burnt-out old places."[27]

But even with a more concerted effort to clear in advance of the flooding, restricted funding and lack of time again limited the effort on Arrow, a situation that would haunt the government in later years.

The water licence for Mica reservoir gave BC Hydro and Ministry of Forests crews ten years to clear the reservoir. With 450 miles of shoreline encircling the reservoir, meeting what seemed like a modest goal was still a challenge. Initially, Hydro crews concentrated on harvesting a narrow band of trees growing on the slope in the planned low-to-high water mark for the reservoir. The terrain was vast, the season short and the funds for such work in a remote area limited by a lack of political will. More logging of the reservoir floor would take place, they hoped, after the completion of the dam, since they had calculated it could take four years to fill. A few

---

[26] Waterfield, *Continental Waterboy.*
[27] Waterfield, *Land Grab.*

big water years followed immediately after completion, resulting in the reservoir filling in half the predicted time. As it filled, unlogged timber loosened its hold and floated to the surface. Other timber roots clung fast to the land, not to loosen until a decade or two later, at which point a tree might shoot up to the surface unexpectedly, startling a fisherman in his boat.

***

We are eating our dinner at the picnic table when a man bikes past to retrieve some fish he has stored in the little creek to keep them cool. On his return, he stops for a visit and explains that he has been coming to Kinbasket reservoir to fish for 20 years. Bob Salant found the spot by scanning a map of BC for any waterways at highway dead ends. He cracks open a beer and settles in to talk. *The fishing is the best at the road's end. I come for several weeks every summer.* Technically, it's against government regulations to settle in for long visits, he explains, but he assures me that the campsite is hardly ever used. He has caught rainbow trout, bull trout, burbot and kokanee. I ask about weather. Has he heard anything about the two boating accidents that happened just after the reservoir was filled, the first involving the drowning of Boy Scouts on a canoe trip? In the second, a fisherman was stranded in an unexpected storm and died of exposure as he tried to swim to shore. No, Salant says, he is not aware of these, but he confirms that he has encountered an array of unlikely and intense weather when out fishing. He is surprisingly philosophical about the danger.

A few times, I wasn't sure I'd survive what the mountains were throwing at me. I'd huddle in the bottom of my boat and wait it out.

He takes a sip of his beer and shakes his head.

You inject this much water into a confluence valley, and it happens.

Listening to his stories of summer hailstorms, dense fog, sharp winds, biting shards of rain and lightning, I realize that the rugged upper Columbia system has not lost its moxie. Settling down to sleep later that night, I recall the starkly worded warning sign we passed as we crested the dam and made our way to the campsite. Bush pilot Kelly Mortensen recently told me at a public meeting that he has experienced winds of 60 knots in the valley, accompanied by violent turbulence unlike any he has ever known. Four major mountain ranges converge at the Big Bend valley: the Rockies, Purcells, Selkirks and Monashees. Three rivers come together here, too: the Wood, Canoe and Columbia. The conditions for a pilot, Mortenson had explained, are capricious to the extreme.

From the descriptions of these two men and the information scattered in the historical record, it's clear that the reservoir can act like a cauldron, with wind from side canyons boiling waves up five feet high. The remote location, limited facilities, extreme water fluctuations and weather have all served to severely limit the growth of recreational tourism originally promised by BC Hydro.

I tune my ears to the water. Outside the tent, the warm August air is almost too still. Only if I strain my ears can I hear the friendly trickle of Potlatch Creek. Reservoirs are empty places, even if the fishing is sometimes good. Mica's fish habitat, fed by many tributary streams high in the mountain system, is somewhat of an anomaly. Fish that have evolved in free-running river systems don't usually go well with captured water.

* * *

During water licence hearings for Duncan and Arrow, conservationists had been clear about the great threat to fish and wildlife that the dams posed. Over 4,500 acres of waterfowl habitat, tens of thousands of acres of winter feeding range and aquatic habitat for migratory bull trout, kokanee and the prized, world-famous Gerrard rainbow were at risk. The water licence for Duncan Dam required BC Hydro to build the two-mile-long Meadow Creek spawning channel immediately downstream of the Duncan Dam in 1967. Further south, on the south shore of Kootenay Lake, Hydro enhanced Duck Lake in the Creston marshlands to partially mitigate waterfowl habitat losses in the Duncan valley. No wildlife mitigation was planned for the Arrow valley, or for Mica.

The BC government estimated the wildlife losses associated with the flooding of Mica in a final report from the BC Environment and Land Use Committee, released in June, 1974, after the completion of the dam. The report acknowledged that the numbers were rough estimates, given the lack of baseline measurements or surveys prior to filling the reservoir: 1,000 acres of permanent wetland, 2,000 acres of seasonal wetland and 950 acres of meadow. Impact on wildlife was estimated have been "severe," affecting 2,000 moose and 3,000 bears and resulting in a "near total displacement" of songbirds, waterfowl, beavers, otters, martens and amphibians. The report concluded: "little opportunity remains in the Mica Basin to replace lost habitat." A later report funded by BC Hydro that analyzed aerial photos taken before the flooding was more scientifically precise: 42,000 hectares (almost 104,000 acres) of aquatic and terrestrial ecosystem, 36 per cent of which was river/riparian forest and

12 per cent of which was wetland. In both cases, these losses from the Kinbasket reservoir represent about half of the total of such habitat lost by all three dams constructed in Canada for the CRT.[28]

The ecologically destructive nature of storage reservoirs is today widely documented and understood. A dam the size and strength of Mica could not possibly have a benign impact on the wilderness valleys that it flooded. Beaver, marten and groundhog; larger mammals such as moose, deer, caribou and bear; raptors, songbirds and amphibians – all lost their homes and their places to browse, hunt or sing.

* * *

Near dawn, the warm stillness finally breaks. I wake to trees whispering and swaying around our two small tents. After breakfast, I return to the beach, where a strong wind has transformed yesterday's sheet of blue-green glass into a ruffled grey skirt. I tuck myself behind a hunk of driftwood and stare out at the agitated surface of the reservoir. Named for a once-high-profile chief of the Secwepemc/Shuswap tribe, the word Kinbasket means "reaching for the highest part of the sky" or "touching the sky."[29] Originally, when the reservoir filled, the BC government named the reservoir McNaughton Lake, after the intrepid general. By the 1980s, it was being labelled Kinbasket Lake on maps.[30]

---

[28] G. Utzig and D. Schmidt, *Dam Footprint Impact Summary: BC Hydro Dams in the Columbia Basin, March, 2011.* Prepared for the Fish and Wildlife Compensation Program: Columbia Basin (Nelson, BC). Available online at http://www.sgrc.selkirk.ca/bioatlas/pdf/FWCP-CB_ Impacts_Summary.pdf.

[29] Shuswap Band. http://www.shuswapband.net.

[30] One theory for the name change, offered by a confidential source

The wind combs through the trees while I absently sift small stones that have gathered in a heap behind the roots of one stump. Among them, a sizable and glittering chunk of mica emerges. I pull apart thin slabs of the layered silicate mineral, working the chunk into ever-finer crystalline sheets until all that remains is a single, transparent piece. I lift it and peer through to the reservoir. The ruffled water blurs into a grey smear. I pull away the sheet of mica and blink hard several times, asking the tears to stop. I stare into the distance toward the flooded location of Boat Encampment, trying to use my imagination to drain away all the impounded water, so that I can see once again the lush, mature riparian and coniferous forest that once existed several hundred feet below me. I imagine splendid white-barked birch and cottonwood, puffs of wetland willow and tangled alder, towering cedar and command-ing pines. (Ships' masts.) Heaps of gravel and silt. (Borrow areas.) A wild, free river, bending south, gathering strength, descending from the Continental Divide. If I didn't know the history, would I think anything had been lost? Will there be an opportunity to give back the silt, sand and gravel? Will trees ever grow here again? I tuck a few ground-up fragments of the glistening mica into my notebook before returning to the campsite to pack up the car.

A few weeks later, some of the mica's silvery glitter-dust drifts away from my journal's gutter and falls onto the desk. I gather up as much as I can and seal it back onto the page with a piece of clear

---

familiar with the process, is that it was a response to criticism from members of General McNaughton's family, who felt that the general's vision for managing the Columbia River system in Canada had been overruled by the CRT and did not want one of its reservoirs named for him. Nothing yet found in the historical record verifies this story.

adhesive tape. Carbon tests of soil taken from near the dam site during construction revealed samples of decayed wood 21,000 years old, proving that the forest there predated the most recent glaciation. Scientific observation begun in the era of Thompson's explorations has flourished in the two centuries since. Science plays an important role today in understanding and maximizing the magnificence of the Columbia River's hydro-power potential. Yet, without any tether to the wild and unbidden heart of a landscape, the rigour of scientific data can stiffen perception and any other values. It can trump the passion that originates from an unseen source, or the mystery expressed in the unknown path that lies ahead.

2. Taking a Stand, Standing in the Way: The Social Complexity of Forced Removal

Lifelong upper Columbia River resident Brian Gadbois has vivid childhood memories of wooden survey stakes painted bright yellow. Playing in the woods along the river just south of Revelstoke, BC, in the early 1960s, he came across some of the stakes marking the future circumference of the High Arrow reservoir's safe line: precisely 1,460 feet (455 metres) above sea level, the elevation below which all property would be expropriated for public good. Seventy feet (21 metres) above the average level of the Columbia River, the stakes could be seen from a distance or followed from one to the other on foot, making it clear to everyone in the community whose land would be lost by the flooding of the valley, and whose land would survive.

The Gadbois dairy farm was below the stakes. Brian and his brother pulled the yellow stakes up whenever they found them, convinced that somehow this defiant act would save their family's land.

It did not. Expropriation involves forced removal through legal action. It is the most extreme form of relocation. The Province of BC flexed its legal muscles, and people had to go. Many landowners did not want to leave their homes in the Arrow Lakes valley. Some, like Christopher Spicer, planted their feet and took a stand against BC Hydro in the court system. Some, like Gadbois's family, resigned themselves, took settlements quietly and moved, though they carried with them seeds of bitterness. When it came to the wrenching separation of agricultural people from their land, there were no right answers to the wrong equation of corporate interests and natural landscapes.

Some of my earliest memories involve visits to my grandparents' ranch in central California. I would bump along in my grandfather's pickup, feeling that I somehow belonged in the oak savannah like he did. These early experiences taught me what it felt like to bond to a landscape. It's a habit that has followed me all my life, no matter where I have lived. Natural places matter. Belonging to them can matter, too. Not just houses or built communities. Places are natural systems. Shorelines. Fields. Forests. Rivers. Meadows. Grazing lands. Gardens. Watersheds. Places are imbued with the particular character of a climate, a strength of wind, a smell of rain, the cast of light across mountains at sunrise.

Does my love of the *love of place* help to open my heart to Brian Gadbois, Janet Spicer and others who tell stories of reluctant departure? Whatever the reason, I am listening, and I don't like what I hear.

It was up to BC Hydro to compensate inhabitants for "irreparable harm" caused by the process of dam construction.[1] Hydro called

---

[1] Wilson.

the process of forcing people to move against their will a "resettlement program."[2] This euphemism masked the complexity and
pain of the real human experience, and the devastating impacts to
the landscape itself. The harm was – and still is, to a large extent
– irreparable.

* * *

BC Hydro appraisers arrived in the upper Columbia region in June
1964 to distribute a cheerful information pamphlet titled *Completion
of the Treaty Dams*. The pamphlet explained with no small measure
of pride that the three large dams would "change the map of British Columbia. Three new lakes will be created, several small communities will disappear … and some new communities will be
established."

As part of the resettlement process, planners working for BC
Hydro decided that a few communities could be moved up from
the area slated to be flooded. In another pamphlet distributed to
residents the following year, BC Hydro emphasized its forward-
thinking approach, expressing an optimistic desire to engage residents in the design of these new communities. The positive aspects
of the treaty were emphasized: employment valued at as much as
$100-million, new highways and bridges, and new townsites at Bur-
ton, Fauquier and Edgewood. The negative aspects – the temporary
nature of most of the employment, the flooded road and rail access,
the destruction of heritage – were not mentioned. Subsequent
newsletters written by BC Hydro and circulated throughout the
region contained tidy drawings of the proposed communities,

---

[2] The US Indian Administration used the identical euphemism when
forcing indigenous people from their traditional lands in the west.

brightly named New Fauquier, New Edgewood and New Burton. A model of modern planning, the street layouts minimized
through-traffic, providing a centrally located commercial centre
and public walkways. The pamphlet suggested the planting of vegetation to screen lots from the new highway. Destruction and forced
removal were being repackaged and marketed to be appealing.

There were other promises in the idealistic plans: three permanent bridges would span the new reservoir, replacing the ferry system.[3] The bold design for the $6-million bridge at Needles would
link the Monashee Highway through the Arrow Lakes valley to
another promise: a brand new highway from Fauquier to Passmore
that followed Koch Creek. "We are designing that bridge right now,"
highways minister P.A. Gaglardi said in Nelson in May 1965."[4] His
statement indicated that it might be under construction before the
dams were finished.

It all looked good on paper. And yet, as Jim Wilson, the man
appointed by BC Hydro to be responsible for the forced removals
said, many years later: "It is one thing to have visions and ideals
for yourself; quite another to have them for others."[5] Anticipating

---

[3] One at Needles, one at Kinnaird, and one crossing the crest of the
High Arrow Dam. Only the latter bridge was completed.

[4] *Arrow Lakes News,* May 13, 1965. With the promised fixed link,
Fauquier appeared to have the best growth prospects of all the
settlements. (*Arrow Lakes News*, February 10, 1966.) BC Hydro
economists also predicted a significant rise in tourist spending
throughout the region, with at least a third of it coming from visitors
who would flock to the dams or recreate on the reservoirs.

[5] At the time of dam construction, Wilson was optimistic about
meeting the deadline of 1969 for resettlement of Arrow Lakes valley
residents. By early 1966, over 500 of 1,600 claims had been settled

the ideals of others had followed quick on the heels of a treaty signed without those "others" being consulted. In the end, BC Hydro acknowledged that "building new communities cannot be a one-sided business.... those who will live in the new communities must first say what they want and be prepared to work with us." As resettlement efforts continued, many residents were unhappy about moving to a place that they had not really chosen. The glow surrounding the New Communities dispersed. To complicate the process further, financial restrictions grew as the financial strain of meeting the project deadlines began to affect the provincial budget. Some of the bright new infrastructure originally promised to the residents would never be built.[6]

In all, over 2,000 households would be uprooted. Only a handful of people lived in the remote valleys behind the proposed Mica Dam. A few hundred lived in the Duncan River valley. The greatest number of affected households was in the Arrow Lakes valley between Revelstoke and Castlegar.

Hugh Keenleyside had stated clearly at the 1961 water licence hearings that people would be bought out at fair market value and that BC Hydro would help them find comparable land on which to farm.[7] According to *The Property Owners' Guide* distributed throughout affected areas, it was BC Hydro's intent to obtain land "not at the lowest possible price but at a fair price." However, the authority also dictated that there would be no "bargaining" or negotiating, leav-

---

already, Wilson said, with only a few formal appropriations at that point and mostly co-operative landowners. "We have been as generous as we can be." (*Vancouver Sun,* January 8, 1966.)

[6] Wilson.

[7] BC Archives, GR0880, Box 16.

ing in its hands entirely the process of arriving at a fair price. In the early days of resettlement, Jim Creighton, a resettlement officer, reported that Hydro "frequently paid more than a property is worth." But the decision to suppress speculative land prices actually created a culture of secrecy as those who sold out early were told that they should not share the price they had received in the community. Residents were reminded of the "rigid time schedule" for constructing the dams under the terms of the treaty, and that a failure to meet the deadlines for project completion would result in penalties paid to the United States.[8]

Some of the stories:

1. Larry and Coreen Greenlaw

As bulldozers revved up and dynamite blasted at the Duncan Dam site, BC Hydro appraisers approached the 20-odd landowners living in Howser, a community of approximately 100 people on the southern shoreline of the 16-kilometre-long (ten-mile) Howser Lake. In 1960, Larry Greenlaw and his wife Coreen had purchased a gas station and store there, on a half-acre triangle of land with 73 metres (240 feet) of lakefront and a floating dock. They had moved into a house just up the hill, set on four town lots that they purchased from Larry's grandfather John Malcolm Greenlaw's estate. John Greenlaw had arrived over half a century earlier, just after the first silver rush in the region. For a time, he had owned a hotel in Lardeau called the Britannia and operated a farm on the lower reaches of Howser Lake – farming potatoes, mowing meadow hay and raising livestock on the rich flood plain soil. The townsite and fertile farmland at the lake's south end were slated to be flooded

---

[8] Quoted in Wilson.

by the construction of the Duncan Dam, which would swallow up Howser lake and make it part of the new Duncan Lake reservoir. Larry's wife Coreen also had deep roots in the upper Columbia basin. Her father, Roy Collier, farmed in the Arrow Lakes valley, at East Arrow Park, a community also slated for flooding. BC Hydro gave Larry and his wife a decent offer early on, as they did to other prominent landowners in Howser like Billy Clark and Doc Wilkinson. The Greenlaws accepted $20,000 for the house on the four city lots, and the 73 metres of lakefront.

The Greenlaws didn't want to sell out but felt helpless in the face of the changes. With their settlement, they invested in a store in nearby Meadow Creek and began to make a living the best way they could. They considered themselves lucky to have received a relatively fair settlement early, as they watched and heard about other residents across the basin struggling to receive just payment for the value of their land. BC Hydro, they heard, appeared to send different agents into a specific area with a set total that they could spend, and whatever was left over, the agent got a percentage. Whether or not these rumours were true, the stories fed an increasing sense of resentment across the region.[9]

2. Ryder and Daisy Havdale

The Havdales purchased three acres of waterfront on the Lower Arrow Lake in 1960. The previous owners of their parcel, the Websters, had owned a large farm there since early in the 20th century. When Mr. Webster's father died, they had decided to subdivide the three-acre portion. The Havdales' new place had over 100 metres (328 feet) of sandy beach, vacation cabins for rental, a large garden and

---

[9] Larry Greenlaw, telephone interview by author, May 2011.

a house. Over a 50-year period, the senior Mr. Webster had developed mature gardens that contained nearly two dozen fruit and nut trees, many large trees and unique flowering shrubs, 58 varieties of roses and a dozen grape vines, as well as flowering perennials and bulbs. Over the next three years, the Havdales poured time and effort into upgrading the house, cabins and gardens. They had no idea that their property sat almost precisely on the spot where the High Arrow Dam would be constructed.

In early June 1964, Daisy Havdale was working in the garden when she heard news that a neighbour's home was on fire. When people rushed to help, they found BC Hydro field men "acting as if they had pulled a hilarious joke … cleaning up the 'mess' and laughing."[10] The Havdales had heard something about a dam being constructed and properties purchased, but no one had yet called on them, and no one in the area had been told that homes being purchased would be burned. One month later, an assessor named Mr. Wiebe called on Daisy and Ryder and offered $5,000 for 102 metres of beach and three acres of land. The Havdales refused. Four days later, rock blasting at the dam site broke three of their windows and knocked dishes from the cupboards. Over the next month, the Havdales received further visits from the BC Hydro negotiator, and verbal offers that gradually increased from $5,000 to $8,000, to $16,000, and finally to $26,000. The Havdales refused and sought an independent valuation of their property, but had difficulty locating anyone in the region who might be willing to do the work. On August 24, field workers surveying for the new road to the dam site turned off their water without permission. A few months later, they finally received an independent appraisal: $60,000.

---

[10] Havdale.

Resettlement officers, most of whom were sent in from outside the region, were unprepared for the emotional distress a forced removal could create. They did not take well to resistance on the part of landowners. Jim Creighton admitted to the hard feelings and resistance that met some BC Hydro land valuators by describing to media how they were greeted by barbed wire and Alsatian dogs. In the case of the Havdales, their resistance to settling quickly was, according to Daisy, answered with trespassing, verbal threats and intimidation from the resettlement officer, in this case, a Mr. Baxter.[11]

In early January 1965, the Havdales received a final offer from BC Hydro of $32,500, with the threat that if it was not accepted by the following day, formal expropriation proceedings would begin. Their neighbours, the Websters, were offered $41,000. Dejected and unable to fight any further, both families finally accepted. The stress for the Havdale family was not over, however. For $16,000, they purchased ten acres subdivided from a farm downstream and to the south, near Robson. Their new property had no waterfront access, no vacation cabins and no mature garden. They wanted to move their home from its site beside the Columbia River to the new property, but this cost would not be covered by BC Hydro. When they were finally resettled later that year, the Havdales were in debt for the first time in their lives.

3. Oliver and Helen Buerge

Like many farming families, Oliver Buerge and his wife Helen were practical and down-to-earth. They were not inclined to resist what they could not control. In 1961, when Oliver heard that the Columbia

---

[11] For more on this story, see Havdale.

River Treaty had been signed, he immediately sold his herd and expected appraisers to call on him soon after that to make an offer on their 190-acre farm on the shores of the Columbia in Burton. When protracted political delays and the uncertainty about the treaty's ratification stretched on into years, he and Helen eventually bought back some cattle and began farming again. In 1966, two BC Hydro appraisers, H.R. Webster and Ken Howard, finally came calling.

Oliver and Helen had both been born and raised in the Arrow Lakes valley. Helen's parents had come from France circa 1900 and settled on land in Burton. Oliver's father had come with Mennonite farmers around the same time. Oliver was born in Needles, just downstream. He purchased 110 acres of flat, fetile, low-lying land just after the Second World War, part of it as a wedding gift for his wife. In 1956, with the help of the Farm Loan Board, he purchased 30 more acres of adjoining cleared land with a fine farmhouse. A few years after that, he purchased 40 more acres of arid land further away from the river. By 1956, he possessed the full 190 acres, with 915 metres (3,000 feet) of beach, and was raising milk cows and cattle for beef. By any objective standard, he could be considered a prosperous farmer.

He had watched his father buy and sell property all his life. Of the 190 acres he owned, 129 were below the proposed flood line, with only ten naturally flooded by the Columbia River each year. This ten-acre parcel had become, with careful management, a highly productive hay meadow mowed twice each season: once before the annual spring flood, and once again after the flood waters had nourished the fields and receded. Of the 129 acres below the new reservoir flood line, 110 were highly fertile and represented more than half the value of the farm.

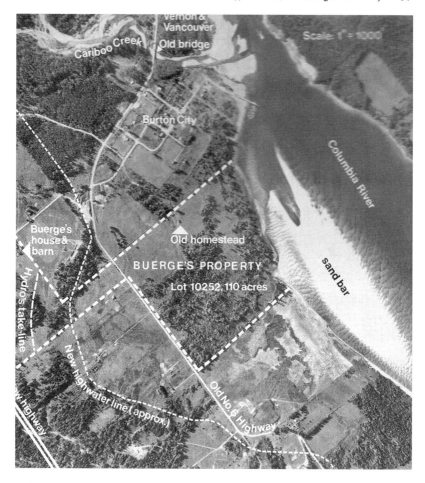

The back cover of Donald Waterfield's book Land Grab shows an aerial view of the Buerge farm. Note the high water mark, indicating lost farmland and the townsite of Burton.

Neither of the appraisers was professionally qualified, but they had so far had a good track record of making many successful deals with people in the Arrow Lakes valley. They offered the Buerges a lump sum of $38,000 for the entire farm, or $16,500 for the 129 acres only, about half the minimum going rate in the 1960s for cleared farmland.

If the Buerges chose the latter option – to retain their house and the 60 arid acres – their new property lines would have had a 122-metre (400-foot) beach on the new reservoir, but only if BC Hydro offered them an easement across their expropriated land, which it did not plan to do. The appraisal of over $21,000 for the house and 60 acres was, in Buerge's estimation, generous. But the extremely low appraisal of the good farmland, and the lack of any value given to the waterfront when he knew that others in the valley had received $12 per foot ($39 per metre), made the total offer unfair in his view. The offer predisposed the Buerges to sell out for a small price. Like their upstream neighbours Christopher and Jean Spicer, they could not replace what they had without a much more generous settlement.

Herein lay one of the key difficulties in the expropriation process. To an agency preparing to flood it, the land had almost no marketable agricultural worth. In other words, what was land worth if it was only going to be flooded? The promise made during water licence hearings by Hugh Keenleyside – replacement value – had been confounded by the continued cost overruns of the construction process. Rationales were flurrying through the air.

Under BC Hydro's stated expropriation policy, residents could contest appraisals, requesting a second opinion on the appraisal. If this, too, was unsatisfactory, residents could challenge the settlement in court. Oliver Buerge received his second appraisal, hired a lawyer and prepared for court. It would be a long and challenging fight, spanning the construction phase of both the High Arrow and Duncan projects, with Buerge's case the only one to go before a judge.

He appeared before judge Charles William Morrow in Vernon, BC, in the autumn of 1968. BC Hydro's aggressive defence of the original appraisal included an attack against Oliver's character. Oliver withstood this, and in June 1970, the court ordered a judgment against BC Hydro – the only one brought about by the expropriation process. BC Hydro had to pay $35,833 for the land below the flood line (with $5 per foot for waterfront), as well as all of the Buerges' costs for lawyers, court documents and independent appraisals. The corporation promptly sent a cheque for a mere $12,000 and then appealed the decision. By late 1970, Oliver Buerge's appeal was no closer to getting under way. Meanwhile, his lawyer, Neil Davidson, had been trying to negotiate with the crown corporation to purchase an easement to the waterfront. BC Hydro had offered to sell the 122 metres of waterfront access to the Buerges at a rate of $40 per foot (approximately $130 per metre), eight times more than the purchase price it had been ordered by the courts to pay to the Buerges. The corporation offered Oliver the money awarded by the judge for his property but nothing for his legal costs. If he accepted, they said, they would abandon the appeal.

The Buerges resisted again. By this time, counsel for the couple was convinced that BC Hydro's procrastination was not motivated by money, given that the sum involved in the settlement was out of proportion to the magnitude of the litigation. The reason for the corporation's stubbornness, Davidson had decided, was pure retribution. A few days before Christmas 1971, and without explanation, BC Hydro finally abandoned its appeal and paid the Buerges all legal and land costs.[12]

---

[12] For more on the Buerge story, see Waterfield, *Land Grab*.

4. Mary and Angus Bajowksy

Another dispute was brewing, this one at the upper reaches of the Arrow Lakes reservoir, just outside of Revelstoke, where the BC Highways Department was offering Mary Bajowsky $1,800 for 5.58 of her 27 acres. The department was relocating the main highway from its original location near the riverbed. Mary's husband, Angus, had purchased it in his wife's name in 1960, only a dozen years after immigrating from Poland. His swift rise from hard labourer to land-owner was a clear testimony to his focus and dedication.

Born Ignatius Bajowsky in the Ukraine in 1924, Angus lived there until he was 16 years old, when the Russian Army swept through the village at night to force young men into service. After the war, he escaped to Germany, and eventually to Canada in 1948, at the age of 24. When he arrived, he spoke no English, but gradually he learned enough to pass exams to become a fireman, then a locomotive engineer. He married Mary Bobyak, a Ukrainian-Canadian who had recently arrived in BC from Alberta. Together, they worked hard, with Angus operating a small farm while he continued to work for CPR, and Mary making cheese, selling eggs and raising children.

Undeterred by the Bajowskys' refusal to sell, the Highways Department began blasting rock on the slope above their home, resulting in a loss of their water source for several months. Fuelled by a strong sense of natural justice, they dug in their heels.

***

In the spring of 1968, the High Arrow Dam was nearing completion. Pressure was mounting on the Bajowskys. Engineers hired by BC Hydro determined that even though the Bajowsky house and much of their land was between the proposed highway and the shoreline of the reservoir, the slope was likely unstable due to deep deposits of sand and silt. In May 1968, the corporation recommended expropriation of more land. In July, BC Hydro offered the couple $18,400 for all the property between the highway easement and the shoreline.[13] Once again, they flatly refused to sell. In August, the local MLA, W.S. King, wrote to BC Hydro on behalf of the Bajowskys, taking "strong issue with unnecessary expropriation with its attendant dislocation and disruption to individual citizens." That same month, BC Hydro arranged for another appraisal[14] that determined the government offers to be fair, and next served notice of expropriation.

In November, 1968, the High Arrow dam was completed, but the Bajowskys were still resisting BC Hydro and the Highways Department. An appropriation valuator named Frederick Cunningham of North Vancouver determined that $24,000 was fair. That same month, Mary Bajowsky wrote to BC Hydro, begging for fair treatment. She knew that the offer was only half the amount a comparable property nearby had received.

Early the following year, Mary made a second request for fair replacement value, land for land.[15] She spoke of illness and stress. BC Hydro replied that they would expropriate and enclosed a cheque for $24,823.55. In February, she wrote to W.A.C. Bennett and enclosed the cheque uncashed. BC Hydro next reported the family to provincial authorities for health violations. They continued calling on the family with requests for them to accept the money and go.

---

[13] BC Hydro to Angus and Mary Bajowsky.
[14] W.S. King to E.S. Collins, August 13, 1968.
[15] Mary Bajowsky to BC Hydro, January 23, 1969.

That spring, the Bajowskys attended the dam's official opening on June 9, 1969. W.A.C. Bennett surprised the audience with an announcement that project would now be called the Hugh Keenleyside Dam, in honour of retiring BC Hydro chairman Hugh Keenleyside. It was, for the government, a success story. Some of Arrow's cost overruns had been gained back by an early completion bonus of C$5-million. The dam had also earned a one-time C$56.3-million flood control payment from the US, the lion's share of the total flood control payment owed to Canada.[16] When Bennett praised BC Hydro directors for what he called "the better life," the ironies were too great for Angus Bajowsky. Standing near the podium he cried out from the audience.

Not for me.

Bajowsky was quickly forced to the back of the crowd by officials. When he approached Bennett at the end of the ceremony, the premier brushed past him, saying, "Not now, not now, come see me in Victoria." Trade and Commerce minister Waldo Skillings shoved Angus away and said, "Oh, get away from here." BC Hydro co-chairman Dr. Gordon Shrum approached Angus at the event and promised an investigation into the Bajowskys' case. Shrum told *The Province* that he "had respect for Bajowsky" for coming right out in the open with his concerns.[17]

---

[16] BC Hydro and Power Authority, *Arrow/Mica Columbia Construction Progress Report No. 16. October, November, December 1968.*

[17] "Hydro's 'Fair Deal' Offer Cuts Compensation $1,000," *Vancouver Sun,* August 1, 1969; "Heckler Dims Socred Sunshine," *Vancouver Sun,* June 10, 1968; "Skillings, Heckler Scuffle as Bennett Dedicates Dam," Vancouver *Province,* June 10, 1969; "Protests, Surprise, Mark Arrow

Several days after the opening of the Hugh Keenleyside Dam, the Bajowskys received an anonymous phone call. "Leave Bennett alone and take what you are getting. Don't cause any trouble or you won't be able to enjoy what you get." Finally, BC Hydro consented to a reappraisal, which only resulted in a slightly lower offer. Mary Bajowsky wrote again to Gordon Shrum, begging for fair treatment. BC Hydro continued to warn them to leave, even as the water rose. One field worker told Mary to "go back to the Ukraine." In October, 1969, the Bajowskys received permission from BC Hydro to stay in the house through the winter, "as a result of lower than normal water levels [having accumulated] during the past summer." This same letter proposed a final offer of $25,000, giving them essentially nothing for the value of the house itself and requesting that they dismantle it at their expense. Exhausted and defeated, the Bajowskys accepted the offer and, with it, negotiated an agreement that if the 15 acres above the reservoir level was eventually deemed safe, they could purchase it back. Angus summarized the threats and intimidation of his wife and family as actions of a Canadian "Gestapo."

In January, 1970, Mary Bajowsky again sought permission to buy her land back and enclosed a deposit. BC Hydro official Earl Moffat called on the family more than once to urge them to give up the first right to repurchase their expropriated land. On March 16, 1976, Mary was able to purchase back the property for $320.50 per acre, plus interest and appreciation of over 50 per cent since

---

Dam Dedication," *Arrow Lakes News,* June 11, 1969; "Revelstoke Man Fights for Land," *Vancouver Sun* (accessed in Arrow Lakes Historical Society archives; date obscured in copy).

the Highways Department had purchased the land from her. This appreciation in the property's value more or less reflected the rate of inflation between 1969 and 1976.[18] After all they had endured, to the Bajowskys, the passing on of this increase from BC Hydro to the original owners felt quite rightly like profiteering.

5. The Morton Family

The Mortons' 360-acre farm included 2745 metres (9,000 feet) of waterfront, a mature cedar and cottonwood forest, and large, productive fields for hay and other crops. Many valley residents remember it as one of the loveliest farms in the valley between the two Arrow Lakes. A large portion of the 360 acres would remain above the flood line, and much of that was filled with forest. Citing concerns about soil stability, BC Hydro purchased the entire farm from the Morton family in the late 1960s. The price they were paid per acre was less than what BC Hydro was paying contractors to clear adjacent land.[19] When they sold, the Mortons were unaware that BC Hydro had been corresponding with the government's Parks Branch since 1964 about the possibility of turning the land above the new high water mark into a provincial park. Direct purchase rather than expropriation of this property was in line with BC Hydro policies at the time – that land should not be expropriated for recreational purposes.[20]

In 1967, Val Morton listed farming activities on the family acreage: 84 head of cattle, with 24 for beef to local market; 140 tons

---

[18] The increase in Statistics Canada's Consumer Price Index between 1969 and 1976 was 53.76 per cent, or, 6.93 per cent per year, compounding.

[19] Nigel Waterfield, interview by author, May 2011.

[20] Morton.

of alfalfa hay; 75 tons of chopped hay in self-feeder; 20 acres fall-plowed and cultivated. In 1968, BC Hydro announced the formation of McDonald Creek Provincial Park. In 1969, Val Morton "felt he was forced to accept $130,000 for the property."[21]

By early spring of 1969, the Arrow reservoir was nearly completed and flooding of the valley had begun. At the proposed highway bridge near Fauquier, BC Hydro had spent nearly $1-million on bank stabilization and driving piles when the government announced that the bridge was being postponed indefinitely. Talk of the new highway along Koch Creek to connect Fauquier with Highway 3 had faded as well. One relocated resident, Ron Volansky, had purchased land on the strength of this proposed highway connection, to construct a hotel in one of the communities to be served by a new bridge. Without a bridge, the tourism value of his new project decreased substantially. [22]

As many of the government's promises to rebuild the region remained unfulfilled, residents increasingly saw the proposals as a false effort to smooth over the dislocation and destruction.[23] The reservoir land that had been adequately or inadequately burned, logged and prepared was still riddled with stumps that regularly caught fishing lines and frustrated anglers. Some stumps had been buried in shallow graves by contractors hired to clear the reservoir, and as the water drew up and down, they worked loose. Instead of providing glorious recreational opportunities, the Arrow Lakes and

---

[21] Ibid.

[22] *Arrow Lakes News,* February 14, 1968; April 14, 1968; May 29, 1968.

[23] *Vancouver Sun,* February 1968. (Accessed in Arrow Lakes Historical Society archives; exact date obscured in copy.)

Duncan Lake reservoirs had destroyed hundreds of natural sandy beaches in the valleys – a loss that residents faced, summer in and summer out, as they attempted to adjust to the new realities of a landscape sold out to corporate water use.

Just a few years earlier, an academic named John V. Krutilla had published an objective economic evaluation of the treaty in which he concluded that it was not clear whether "the returns of Canada and the United States combined" were any greater "than they would have been if each country had proceeded independently." In addition, he identified that by 1963, High Arrow had no longer been required to forestall an imminent power shortage. Calling attention to the questionable economics of the Libby, Duncan and Arrow projects, he drew the measured conclusion that "international agreements between riparians should not seek to address planning and operating details." However, with Mica Dam under construction and Libby Dam still to come, Krutilla's analysis, like Richard Deane's several years earlier, made no difference to the catastrophic reality of the Canadian megaprojects in the upper Columbia River watershed.

3. Whittled Down to the Bone: The Lost Landscape of the Upper Kootenay River Valley

I've come to the Touchstones Nelson Museum and Archives at the request of Stanley Triggs, a documentary photographer who recorded the Kootenay River valley and its ranches before the completion of Libby Dam and the flooding of the upper river basin. The museum has recently constructed a website to preserve and display his photographs.[1] I have seen the images online, but Triggs wants to meet me and show me the prints.

I'm old school, he says to me on the phone. *Prints have a certain kind of life to them.*

He greets me when I step off the elevator into the archives. Still fit and vital in his eighties, he has a firm handshake, and his eyes

---

[1] Touchstones Nelson Museum, "Changes Upstream — The Photographs of Stanley G. Triggs." http://touchstonesnelson.ca/exhibitions/triggs/.

dance with a creative spark. I like him immediately, though I could have predicted it. We sit at one of the research tables and Triggs pulls forward two wide, shallow, black portfolio boxes that hold the prints of all the photos he took nearly half a century ago. I don't anticipate that I will learn anything new from seeing the prints in person. My notebook is open beside me, just in case.

***

The US gave formal notice to Canada of their intention to construct Libby Dam on January 27, 1966. Most of the Kootenay River valley land to be flooded in BC was arid, yet rich. Some farmers and ranchers irrigated and farmed the land; others mowed the wild hay and grazed cattle. One-third of the area to be flooded in the US was of a similar character, and the rest was wild, steep canyon. The planned reservoir would have storage capacity of 5.8 MAF and would provide flood control for the agricultural communities of Bonners Ferry, Idaho, and Creston, BC. Ironically enough, one cornerstone of the treaty that resulted from McNaughton's long resistance to Libby in the IJC – the equal sharing of downstream benefits for the life of the treaty – did not apply to this particular project. All benefits from Libby would be retained by the country in which they occurred, as would all compensation for losses. Canada and BC would not receive any downstream hydro-power credits or be reimbursed for the costs of reservoir preparation, including the purchase of land from displaced residents.

Word of the American intention to build the dam was released in 1966 into an upper Columbia region already reeling from the effects of expropriation and reservoir preparation in the Duncan and Arrow valleys. Well acquainted with the national and international controversy over the treaty by now, many residents viewed the development of the Libby Dam as yet another sellout to their local interests.

Federal Canadian treaty negotiators knew at the time the treaty was signed that regulation of the flow of the upper Kootenay River between its headwaters and Kootenay Lake, combined with regulation of in-flow from the Duncan-Howser drainage, would make another downstream Canadian project possible – the Kootenay Canal Generating Station, west of Nelson, BC. This reciprocal if optional benefit for BC is part of the complex nature of the Libby project, one that matches the project's complex trans-boundary geographical setting. In addition, Libby would provide flood control for Creston's agricultural community, though only as a by-product of flood control for nearby Bonners Ferry.

Local industry did not consider Libby to be a sellout as McNaughton had, largely because the Kootenay Canal Generating Station had been an idea floating around the region for years. Dennis A. Williams, the editor of the *Trail Daily Times* and a strong booster of the Libby project, produced a promotional pamphlet about the dam in 1966. As a pro-industry resident of Trail, he supported the American dam on the lower Kootenay River, where Cominco's subsidiary, West Kootenay Power, already operated several profitable run-of-the-river generating plants. He and others assumed that this proposed generating station would one day be owned and operated by Cominco.

Williams claimed that the land to be flooded by the Koocanusa reservoir in BC was "some of the most useless ... in the province ... rocky, overgrazed range, scrub-cattle owned by sub-marginal farmers."[2] He suggested that a good number of the Canadian farmers

---

[2] *Trail Daily Times,* April 1966.

relied on "Christmas-tree cutting and social welfare payments for subsistence" and dismissed the arid ponderosa pine ecosystem as "acres of jack pines not worth the cost of harvesting ... No one need get excited about the prospects of the loss of 42 miles of East Kootenay scrub land when so much prosperity will result at Creston."

Wilson's polemic unfairly categorized the agricultural heritage of the valley as marginal. Several of the landowners in the BC portion of the proposed reservoir had, in fact, farmed for three generations. Over 5,000 head of cattle grazed on several prosperous ranches. As news of the US intent to build the Libby project reached the local level that summer, ranchers formed the Libby Reservoir Property Owners Association. Its chairman, Lloyd Sharpe, owned 876 acres and leased 871 more of Crown land to graze 300 head of cattle. The Waldo Stockbreeders Association and the Fernie and District rod and gun clubs sent a brief to the BC government with regards to the Libby Dam and its effects on the Kootenay River basin.

No one in the BC government acknowledged the brief. Despite the CRT having specifically authorized the Libby project, since it was only an option, not a requirement, the provincial government's position was that it was not actually a treaty project. While residents would have expected BC Hydro to be involved, the government handed over responsibility of expropriation and resettlement to two ministries: Highways and Natural Resources.

***

News of Libby Dam reached Stanley Triggs in 1969, when he was living in Montreal. Born and raised in Nelson, BC, he had returned regularly for years to enjoy summer holidays along Kootenay Lake and the upper Kootenay River. He realized that 25 ranching communities in Canada and one in the US would be flooded or affected; the beautiful Kootenay River landscape he had known would be forever altered. His search for an arts grant to finance the project was unsuccessful, so he did what I would have done. He took his family on a camping holiday.

***

After one landowner's early appeal of an expropriation resulted in a more generous settlement than the Highways Department had offered, the government backed away from the forced removal strategy. A long stare-down with landowners began. Grazing permits that had been issued on a ten-year basis for decades were being offered annually. Operators were encouraged to reduce their inventories. The standard tool for valuing ranching operations, the "cow unit," was dismissed. All of these changes affected property value. On the US side, in the state of Montana, 80 per cent of the settlement offers were paid on signing and the remainder after the property had been vacated. But the Canadian property owners would receive no proceeds until they had left, which made the purchase of new land somewhere else extremely difficult.[3]

BC natural resources minister Ray Williston had promised landowners that the government would make Crown land located above the flooded elevation available for purchase. When the promise materialized, it was in the form of five-acre forested lots with marginal agricultural value, near Baynes Lake and priced at $200 per acre. This was a steep increase over the $35 to $75 per acre that most landowners had been offered for their river-bottom land.[4]

---

[3] Baynes Lake Senior Book Club, *South Country History Book.*
[4] Baynes Lake Senior Book Club, *South Country History Book.*

The ranchers, just as the farmers in the Arrow Lakes valley had been, were caught in a horrible bind.

***

We haven't even started looking at the photos yet, but my pen races across the page of my open notebook. Triggs draws from a deep well of historical knowledge and local experience. This is the best kind of research. Listening to those who have been there, those who know the smells, sights and rhythms of a landscape's past.

Triggs took his first photographs of the Kootenay River valley in the summer of 1969, encountering suspicion from landowners. Those being forced from their ranches and farms understandably mistrusted outsiders. One day, when Triggs stopped on a public road to take a few shots of a ranch house below him, a "burly gentleman" limped up his driveway, bellowing and waving his cane. Initially alarmed, Triggs soon discovered that Bill Ostreich had come not to threaten him but to put in a request. Gradually, word was getting out that the man driving up and down gravel roads with a camera was interested in documenting what would be lost. Rather than chase him away, Ostreich asked Triggs if he could climb up to the benchland behind the ranch to capture a favourite view of the valley.

***

The 16-by-20 inch prints are much larger than I had expected. They come to life under Stanley's touch. He shuffles, stops, holds one up, admires it, tells a story and then lays it down again. The people – long ago aggrieved – and the landscape – long ago flooded – come to life in a way I have never experienced in all my years of researching the history of the upper basin. I am entranced – both by the beauty of the landscape and by the startling dimension and drama of the black-and-white images.

The Ostreich ranch was the first one across the bridge from Waldo – a large river-level ranch that dated back to the earliest days of agricultural settlement by the White family and possessed the oldest log building in the area. Bill had raised two sons to be ranchers. His daughter had also married a rancher. By the time Triggs encountered him waving his cane, Bill had passed on the hardest work to his sons due to complications from Lou Gehrig's disease. He spent days producing leather goods: bridles and hackamores, bullwhips, braided reins, chaps and moccasins. With Triggs, he shared his family's history of the land that he had grown to love. He was not alone.

That first summer, Triggs met the people one by one who lived along the 70 kilometres (43 miles) of Kootenay River from the mouth of the Bull River near Waldo to the US border, in what they called the "South Country." Though it was north of the international boundary, the region was the southernmost part of the Kootenay River basin. The Desrosiers raised grain and hay for 300 head of cattle and 200 head of pigs on 367 acres at Sand Creek and had been in the region since the late 19th century. Across the water, Bob Totten had a ranch of a similar size. Jack Aye had 786 acres and 200 head of cattle. Anton Rosicky owned 1,000 acres and 200 head of cattle. Leo Traska had 240 acres of land on which he grew hay and oats. He had arrived in 1920 after serving for Canada in the First World War, and both of his sons had served in the Second World War. The Sandbergs had farmed near the confluence of the Elk and Kootenay rivers for over 50 years. In all, there were 32 Canadian ranching families, many with long ties to the area.[5] Triggs photographed them all.

---

[5] Baynes Lake Senior Book Club, *South Country History Book.*

I met the people as I recorded them. I came to understand what was at stake. I documented a tremendous loss.

These are not just photographs. They record emotion in a way that stops time. They capture a moment. I am reminded that the human eye is the first camera.

***

The ranchers struggled to achieve fair treatment from a province whose resources were still focused mightily on the Two Rivers Policy, with the valley upstream of Libby Dam falling off the side of government desks. Government agents appeared to have dismissed the 17,600 acres of bottom land as marginal even before the process got underway. Lloyd Sharpe valued his large operation at $230,000, less than replacement cost. He was offered $147,000. Jack Aye was offered $94,000 for his 786 acres and heritage log home, which was later raised to $108,000, both figures well below the assessment of an independent appraiser. Anton Rosicky was offered $86,000 for 1,000 acres, less than half the appraised value. Jack Aye learned that the government had paid the Canadian Pacific Railway $3.2-million for their land, leaving only $1.3-million for private land acquisition – far less than the $7-million that fair compensation would require. Peter Graham, the Cranbrook lawyer retained by the government to oversee the settlement process, told residents at a public meeting that he was "working to make sure that fair settlements are made and that taxpayers' money is used wisely. It is not my function to play Santa Claus."[6]

---

[6] *South County History Book.* The BC provincial ombudsman, Karl Friedmann, oversaw the last settlement for Canadian property owners

In the US, many landowners in the towns of Gateway, Rexford, Warland and others also experienced a dismissive attitude. When they resisted, things did not go well. Jim Kuchinski, whose father and grandfather had homesteads in the valley, can recall stories of his father running government engineers off his land, only to have them return later and threaten the farmer to accept their offer or face the condemning and seizing of the land.[7]

***

They whittled those people down to the bone, Triggs says sadly as he puts down a photo of Bill Ostreich's leather workshop. *What they got paid for their land was criminal.*

In the summer of 1970, Triggs returned to the Kootenay River valley to photograph more people. In a small rowboat, he drifted south down the Kootenay River toward the dam, musing in journals about the terrain around the narrow river channel. The land was hot, arid and open. The river flowing between its dry folds was luscious and cool. The splendid beauty of the watershed continued to move Triggs deeply, though he was not suffering any illusions that what he photographed was pristine. He knew enough of the region's history to understand that the appealing landscape had, like the Arrow Lakes and Duncan River valleys, already experienced the effects of mining and industrial logging. The river, he scribbled in his journal, was like a woman of ill repute who had been treated with great disrespect. He began to see the small-scale ranchers

---

in the Kootenay River Basin in 1985, to a woman whose 77 acres had been flooded 12 years earlier.

[7] Jamison.

and dry-land farmers as people making her respectable again. The ranchers mowed wild hay that never needed to be plowed or seeded. They respected and accepted the river's ups and downs as a natural rhythm to work within. They grazed their animals lightly. Under modest irrigation, the land could also provide good crops of grain, hay or potatoes. It was a good life, and a gentle one.

Triggs lifts up a photo of a young man in leather chaps standing in front of an old log cabin, his horse on one side, his dog on the other. *Cowboy Gordon. Bill Ostreich's eldest son.*

A striking young man. I marvel at the iron strength of his legs, obvious even through the denim and leather chaps he wears. Triggs has recorded a cowboy's solidity, his connection to the ground. He's got all the appeal and earthiness of every rancher I have ever known.

Trigg's voice is thick with admiration.

Gordon had integrity. He chose to bulldoze his own home, rather than let strangers destroy it. Others did the same.

Triggs describes Gordon as shy and deeply attached to the ranch he had been raised on. He sets the photo down and next describes how ranchers disposed of their farm machinery. Some donated their plows and mowers to the Fort Steele historical site. Others followed government orders to dig a trench well under the expected high water mark of the reservoir, drag the machinery into it, and backfill with dirt.

Gordon's father died only three days after signing away their land to the BC government.

He shuffles for another photograph. I put my hand up.

Stan, wait. Can we go back to Cowboy Gordon?

Triggs pulls forward the photo again. Gordon stands beside his horse, an Appaloosa named Coco. At his feet is Buddy, his dog. In his eyes is all the pain of forced dislocation. I can't take my own eyes off the reality of converting river valleys into reservoirs. It's all there.

Triggs moves on to a picture of the Ostreich ranch, looking east toward the Rocky Mountains. Triggs describes how the ranch itself sat on a plateau just above the Kootenay's main channel, with the hayfields naturally irrigated by the river.

It was all wild hay. Dry farming, they call it. Cut and bale. That was all.

He pulls forward another photo – this one a bird's-eye view of another hayfield. The hay has been mown, and the windrows flow like current across the fields.

I climbed a tree to get that shot.

There are more: Anton Rosicky, standing next to a wire fence at the edge of a hayfield. A Mr. McGuinness in his garden. An old truck loaded with a leaning pile of hay in bales, driven by two teenagers. A modest farmhouse close to the international boundary, the wood frame building emerging from a stand of ponderosa pine. Triggs explains to me how he returned reluctantly for his fourth summer of documentation in 1972, knowing that the reservoir would already be half-filled.

I didn't want to face it. A barren desert which had, the last time I'd seen it, been a lush, productive valley. But I forced myself.

He pauses to hold up an image of the destroyed Ostreich home lying in a heap just above the level of the water, with shards of unburned wood sticking out.

Monstrous, isn't it? Like a giant finger pointing to the sky.

The images Triggs took in this last year are haunting but still beautiful: barren piles of gravel, a sandhill crane sloughing in the turgid water, young Cowboy Gordon again, this time riding his horse across his family's partially flooded home pasture. Triggs finds an image out of order, of a garden, this one from the previous summer: squash leaves flopping like open umbrellas with lush potatoes pushing up around them.

Traska's garden. They held out to the bitter end, that family. Finally moved with the water lapped up around their door. Their 240 acres were entirely underwater before government agents had fully negotiated the purchase.

He stands over the stack of images and shuffles through the photos as he explains the process of documentary photography.

It's not fiction, Eileen. It's straight. I draw the feelings out in my subject. I don't interject myself. Sure, my emotions are involved. How could they not be? But I don't let the emotions override the subject itself.

He recalls developing the images back in his Montreal darkroom, watching something he calls "overflow" emerge from the chemical bath.

I manipulated the timing on the process to draw the most out of the image. The mysterious part of it. As I try different approaches, I watched the overflow come through. The emotion. Digital images are flat. Depth and tone are missing, as far as I am concerned.

***

Lincoln County, Montana, also faced significant challenges as construction got underway: the town of Rexford had to be moved. Public services were severely strained by the influx of over 2,000 workers and their families to the rural region. Those living in the region also criticized the federal government for acquiring private land outside of the reservoir area to use as recreation sites that would neutralize the controversy over flooding. After complaints by the county government, the Army Corps of Engineers stepped up to build classrooms, fund the reconstruction of a new junior high school and support the relocation of Rexford.[8] Yet the economic benefits of the operation of Libby still have not made their way back to the region to compensate the lost community. To this day, old-timers on the US side who remember the river describe it as a productive waterway full of fish, friendly to farmers and overflowing with natural beauty. Gerald Marvel, whose father settled in Rexford in 1902, describes the Libby reservoir by comparison as "that damn mudhole." He speaks of the 1948 flood not in terms of destruction but in terms of the large deposits of silt on his fields that brought him a bumper crop of hay that year.[9] "The most beautiful piece of this country," Marvel says, is now "underwater."

In BC, the provincial government had hoped that Kikomun Creek Park on the banks of the new Koocanusa reservoir would appease public controversy over the Libby project. But in the early years of its operation, landslides caused by steeply fluctuating water levels made the reservoir unappealing and often unsafe for boaters. In addition, pollution from upstream Canadian industry[10] threatened water quality and the restoration of fish.[11]

* * *

I say goodbye to Stan and step from the museum into the crisp autumn light. The shadows on the mountains are long, the slopes

---

[8] Spritzer.

[9] Jamison.

[10] Crestbrook Forest Industries in Cranbrook, coal mining in Fernie.

[11] Van Huizen.

aflame with golden-needled larch trees. Landscape, like the people who inhabit it, has its own emotional contours. I can feel melancholy in the air. Mountains, rivers, meadows, deserts – they all catch light and hold beauty in unpredictable ways. Those who live in a place have a way of absorbing that beauty into their bones.

Picking Up the Pieces

1. Reservoir Rye

In 1974, the tenth anniversary of the ratification of the CRT took place in a political atmosphere of doubt and conflict. Two years earlier, W.A.C. Bennett had lost his first provincial election since 1952, to Dave Barrett's environmentally oriented New Democratic Party (NDP). After the election, ongoing public concern over the costs of constructing the dams,[1] and the fact that only one of the three CRT dams in Canada had included plans for generators, fed a polarized debate about whether or not Canada should approach the US about renegotiating the treaty. In this atmosphere, Hugh Keenleyside, retired chair of BC Hydro, published a strongly worded response to the criticism. He argued that even though the projects had gone over budget and did not contain generators, their construction

---

[1] Wikipedia, "Columbia River Treaty/Impacts."

would "make it possible to build additional generating plants in the Columbia River basin in Canada at a much lower cost than creating these projects independently would have done." Under the heading of "Environmental Effects," Keenleyside pointed out that "Duncan Lake used to be almost inaccessible, a swampy morass which was visited by only a few score of people each year" and was now "one of the most beautiful lakes in British Columbia."[2]

For residents in the region, evidence of a recreational paradise was slow in making itself known. Duncan reservoir was still being cleared of trees and other debris to allow safe boating. The *Nelson Daily News* reported that in the Arrow Lakes valley, "tourists on the Keenleyside reservoir have developed a strong aversion to its very poor characteristics, boating over sharp rocks barely covered, no pleasurable beaches or creek fan-outs to stop at, and piles of debris all over."[3] Local governments in the Arrow Lakes valley struggled to get BC Hydro to remove stumps and install boat ramps, as it had promised to do. Mica reservoir had filled in only two years, due to high snow packs after its completion. The surface of the rapidly rising water was so full of logs and other debris that it more closely resembled a log boom than a new recreational lake.[4]

The completion of Libby Dam in 1975 marked the end of direct construction related to the CRT. At the same time, a public intolerance for ecologically damaging megaprojects in North America

[2] Keenleyside, "Ten Years Later: The Results of the Columbia River Treaty." In 1974, Simon Fraser University also sponsored a series of lectures on the CRT. The tapes from these lectures have recently been transcribed and digitized by BC Hydro.

[3] *Nelson Daily News*, September 20, 1976.

[4] *Nelson Daily News*, May 30, 1973.

was growing. Back in 1962, the publication of Rachel Carson's *Silent Spring* had given birth to a new awareness of human impacts on the health of natural systems. US environmental policy had shifted even before Libby was completed, with the National Environmental Policy Act (1969), and consequently an impact statement was required for Libby Dam. The Environmental Protection Agency was created in 1970 and the Endangered Species Act passed in 1973. The Earth First! movement was also fostering an increased awareness of a new science, branded "ecology," which saw the natural world as a web of interconnections. Human beings were within the web, not on top of a heap. Hierarchical views of natural systems were disappearing. Dams were going out of style.

The controversy over the CRT in British Columbia was eventually neutralized by the 1975 election of W.A.C. Bennett's son Bill. Bennett Jr.'s conservative and pro-business policies ensured a second era of construction for the upper Columbia system and oversaw the release for public sale of many parcels of unused land that had been expropriated for the treaty dams. Rather than appease the residents of the Arrow Lakes valley, this liquidation of BC Hydro holdings stirred up the old resentments. Because of inflation, residents would be paying top dollar for land expropriated for minimal amounts. One resident, Garth Belanger, had 42 acres purchased by BC Hydro in 1965 for $9,000. A similar piece of land offered to him just over a decade later would cost $70,000–$90,000.[5]

In the late 1970s and early '80s, despite the growing unpopularity of megaprojects and the lingering bitterness and betrayal in the flooded valleys, BC Hydro quietly initiated and completed three

---

[5] *Nelson Daily News*, January 2, 1979.

additional projects on the original 1960s planning books: the Kootenay Canal Plant (1976), Seven Mile Dam (1979) and Revelstoke Dam (1984), all of which had been made possible by the first three "treaty" dams. As Keenleyside had promised, these dams and generating stations created greater efficiencies in the hydro-electric system by making use of the existing storage from the CRT dams. In addition, BC Hydro installed the first power generators in Mica Dam.

It was during this next decade of dam construction on the Columbia and its tributaries that the dust really started to kick up in the region about the ecological reality of storage reservoirs.

***

I pick my way across reservoir silt, shrugging deeply into my coat collar to escape a raw April wind. Although the calendar says that spring has arrived, snow is still piled high on the majestic mountains rising around me. At my feet, the shifting soil exposed by the annual spring drawdown of the Arrow reservoir gives way unpredictably. Here and there, clumps of dormant reed canary grass form a lumpy mattress of vegetation.

Ahead of me is Brian Gadbois, director of the Dust Control Program for BC Hydro. "Dust control" refers to the planting of annual ryegrass on reservoir silt to limit the late-winter dust storms that plagued the upper reaches of the Arrow Lakes valley after it was transformed into a storage reservoir. As I follow him across this unorthodox farm field, he recalls the first year he and his crew tried to seed the annual rye. It was April 1987 when they drove their pickups onto the reservoir floor. They had delayed planting as long as they could, until the snow was gone and the ground had softened.

They didn't dare wait any longer, though. They knew the grass seeds needed time to germinate and establish before the reservoir filled again with the year's melt.

Gadbois explains how he and his team parked just above the area slated for planting. It was broad daylight, but they left the headlights on to help them see through the dense clouds of dust kicking up into the wind. They had been instructed to plant any exposed area between 1,410 and 1,420 feet (430 and 433 metres). This was more than 20 feet (six metres) below the high water determined by the Columbia River Treaty, 1,444 feet (440 metres),[6] and more than 20 feet above the river's original channel. Having grown up in the valley, Gadbois knew that the land they were planting with ryegrass had once been a dairy farm with fields of mixed grains and grazing animals. Grass would once again be a lifeblood here, but only to quell the dust of public outrage.

***

Around the region, a gap had widened between the optimistic predictions BC Hydro had offered in the early years after ratification and the stark reality of living with a storage reservoir system. No one had thought about the full, long-term effects of a water cycle that is in many ways the reverse of the natural one. The CRT flow requirements caused deep drafting of reservoirs each spring, exposing stumps, forgotten timber and muddy reminders of farms gone by. Promised boat ramps were slow to materialize. Stumps caught fishing lines and wreaked havoc with boaters. Tourists stayed away.

---

[6] The CRT actually authorizes a level up to 1,446 feet, but only with specific permission from the US.

Revelstoke felt the effects of the Treaty in an unpleasant and unpredicted way. Sediment washing into the system from tributary rivers – as well as the soil from the original river shoreline – shifted and moved as the reservoir was filled and drained and filled and drained. By the mid-1970s, the former Columbia River riparian between Revelstoke and Shelter Bay had become swirling dunes of mud, silt and sand, and no riparian vegetation could survive under these unnatural conditions. In late winter and early spring each year, when BC Hydro drained the reservoir to prepare for spring flooding, the valley's winter winds collided with the spreading dunes of silt and created dust storms. The dense, stinging silt filled people's mouths and bit at their cheeks.

But these were no average dust storms. They were an airborne memory of the three dams that had so drastically altered the ecology and human cultural experience of the region. As the dust flew thicker through the 1970s and into the '80s, the construction of Revelstoke Dam also stirred up the old resentments.[7] A general feeling of unrest toward dams and BC Hydro spread south all the way to Castlegar, where Montreal Engineering's final project on the drawing board from the 1957 report – the Murphy Creek Project – received a less-than-enthusiastic response from the community. Complaints about the dust in Revelstoke Reach eventually grew so loud and insistent that they were heard in BC Hydro's head office in Vancouver. The corporation held public meetings in Revelstoke beginning in the mid-1980s.

---

[7] For details on this controversial time for BC Hydro, see Stanley.

***

I stop with Brian in the middle of a wide expanse of reed canary grass (*Phalaris arundinacea*). A Eurasian grass that thrives at the edges of lakes and streams, it was introduced to North America through agriculture but today is widely considered to be invasive. However, Brian stands with his hands shoved deep into the pockets of his lined jacket and praises the plant. A feature of industrial sites, it thrives in poor soils such as reservoirs. It adapts readily to challenging circumstances and can be mown as a feed crop. When I tell Brian that I have read that this one plant can alter entire ecosystems, he laughs.

Yes, Eileen. So can dams.

We walk past the reed canary grass and approach the elevation close to the water's edge, where he and his crew had planted the ryegrass a few weeks earlier. He recalls one speaker in particular at the public meetings, someone who had lived through all the changes brought by the dams. Facing the BC Hydro officials who had flown in from corporate head office to lead the consultation, the speaker made a desperate request.

You've taken away our water and you've taken away our land. Please don't take away the air that we breathe, too.

Brian stoops to have a look at the seeds planted a week earlier.

We had grudgingly accepted the dams by the '80s, Eileen. But we were done with enduring the negative effects. It was about that time, at the public meeting about the dust issue, that BC Hydro finally started to listen to us.

***

Soon after the difficult public meeting in Revelstoke, BC Hydro developed a simple idea: plant a field of grain on the floor of the reservoir. Get it sprouting and growing, then let it be flooded by rising water. The hope was that the root system of the plant would hold the silt in place and, the following year, reduce the dust.

***

Gadbois inspects the new growth of the rye, already over an inch high. Looking every bit a farmer as he crouches close to the ground, he explains how he learned early on that an equal weight of fertilizer must accompany each pound of fall rye seed, to encourage rapid growth in challenging conditions. In the cold wind and rains of early April, the seeds can take up to a week to sprout. Once they do, they need all the help they can get.

Fall rye is pretty hardy stuff. It can survive light spring snowfalls. We want it to grow as much as possible before they start filling the reservoir again.

A natural annual spring flood in a watershed is like breathing. Flood waters move up the river channel and over into the flood plain like oxygen inhaled and then, after a brief pause at the top (in May, June or early July), they exhale back across the flood plain, reducing the river channel as the snowmelt drains to the sea. Reservoir systems, especially storage reservoirs, are a breath inhaled and held for a long, long time. Engineers keep storage reservoirs at or near full pool as long as possible, because this is what gives them the flexibility and reliability they need to create hydro-electricity. The water stays high throughout the growing season, when there is less demand for electricity. During midsummer, the riparian area that would have been exposed again in a natural system remains flooded. As the water passes through the dams to generate power through the fall and the winter, the riparian shoreline gradually comes up for air. By then, the weather has grown cold again and is moving toward winter dormancy.

Sunlight cannot penetrate far enough through the level of "full pool" to feed shoreline plants. The rising and lowering of water, along with wave action from winds, scours the soil near the high water mark, making it hard even for plants at the upper end of the shoreline to establish and prosper. Any submerged aquatic plants that might have tried to take hold when the water was higher cannot next survive the wintertime exposure. A dead zone emerges.

Gadbois and I climb back into his truck and travel north to Revelstoke on a highway crossing a bluff a few hundred feet above the riverbed. Below me are the former riparian areas that once surrounded the Columbia's main channel: the farms, wetlands, natural back-eddies, shallow sloughs for waterfowl and cottonwood forests of lively variety. Today, the forgotten landscape flushes pale green with newly sprung ryegrass. With the water this low, it's easy to see the Columbia's original channel as it winds and swirls through the reservoir rye fields.

The CRT forced Brian to give up the idea of being a farmer. Demonstrating remarkable resilience, he went to work for the corporation that had destroyed the family land. Little did he know that the corporation would one day pay him to farm again – planting a crop destined every year to be drowned. He describes that first dusty, chaotic year of the Dust Control Program, how the crew unloaded tractors and drilling machines, shipped in from a distance since no one local owned or operated much farming equipment anymore. They hooked a drilling machine up behind a tractor and passed it over the silt in the dim, dust-filled light.

It was a surreal experience.

No one knew if it would work. They hoped that the seeds would germinate and grow quickly, gathering the fine silt around their roots to keep it from flying into the air. Theoretically, the following winter and early spring, when the drained reservoir floor would be exposed again, there would be less dust. The rye-planting was a wild, stab-in-the-dark attempt to turn airborne acrid silt into a green and living success. And, unbelievably, it worked.

After a few years, the air began to clear. The Dust Control Program expanded and grew more refined, doubling its acreage in three years and then tripling it in a few more after that. By 2004, BC Hydro was providing up to $250,000 annually for the program, seeding nearly 2,500 acres of reservoir bottomland with fall rye seed. Machines spread 45 kilograms (100 pounds) of fertilizer and 45 kilograms of seed on each acre every year. The fall rye sprouted each spring like a miracle, holding the soil in place more and more firmly. Clearing the air.

At the same time, BC Hydro was also growing more refined in its operation of the reservoir. The CRT required that the corporation deliver a certain amount of flow to the Americans. However, trade-offs with the American system now required additional flows in the spring and summer to support revitalization of the salmon protected by law by the Endangered Species Act, which allowed BC Hydro to reduce the extreme variation in the drawdown.[8] Projections on which elevations to mark out for planting began in early winter, as the snow levels accumulated and technicians predicted how much the reservoir would have to be drawn down to

---

[8] See also BC Hydro's Non-Treaty Storage Agreement, which manages greater efficiencies in the upper Columbia hydro-electric system.

accommodate the coming snowmelt. BC Hydro wanted to plant only as much as it needed to, keeping costs down. In 2001, unpredictably low snowfall and a dry spring translated into a much lower level for the reservoir than had been predicted. So low was it compared to projections that a significant stretch of the fall rye never flooded over that year. It grew, matured and was ultimately harvested as grain to feed animals. Telling me the story, Gadbois seems particularly proud of this weather-assisted outcome for the reservoir farm he was managing.

The planting of ryegrass was intended to control dust, but after almost two decades, Gadbois and others could see that something else had started to happen on the Revelstoke Reach. Water and land, put through a nasty divorce, had begun to reconcile. The air had cleared completely in the community of Revelstoke. The uppermost portion of the long reservoir formed behind High Arrow/Hugh Keenleyside Dam looked decidedly different. Of the 20,000 acres flooded by the dam, over 2,500 blushed soft green in spring, sending up shoots of fall rye 4 to 12 inches high before the flood covered them again. Ten thousand more acres remained barren only at the lowest elevations. This still-unplanted area was the old river channel, combined with the back channels, ponds and un-vegetated flats that before the construction of the dam had reared young fish, hosted waterfowl nests, fed the beavers fresh bark and kept the martens busy.

The remaining 5,500 acres had begun to support natural riparian vegetation, established as a result of the Dust Control Program, or planted by the program with supplemental funding. Gadbois could see that once the fall rye had been inundated every year, its utility did not die with it. The texture and fibres of the plant remain, producing measurable amounts of organic material through the decay of roots and shoots. The persistent replanting of the grass over two decades resulted gradually in greater moisture retention and more stable soil, both hallmarks of a natural riparian system. Clumps of indigenous sedge returned and spread into back channels. Reed canary grass spread like wildfire. BC Hydro began to experiment with regularly harvesting the expanses of canary grass annually as crop feed, to see whether the native grass could survive both flooding and harvest, in much the same way that a natural wetland meadow can be "hayed" by a farmer. Some years, the ryegrass plantings almost resembled Oliver Buerge's pre-CRT shoreline hay meadows near Burton.

In the mid-1990s, just under a decade after the first planting of fall rye, the Friends of Mount Revelstoke and Glacier National Parks established a songbird census program on the Revelstoke Reach. The netting and banding station in the reach captured such a large number of songbirds that the province-wide protocol for allowable birds in the net had to be amended for that station to function. In the spring and fall, Gadbois and others were seeing measurable numbers of waterfowl migrating through the river channel, a sight that was rare before the fall rye planting program began.

And yet the story is not all positive. The return of these waterfowl to a more inviting area means that operations of the reservoir often flood waterfowl nests prior to the fledglings being ready, a reminder that fish and wildlife native to a region always struggle when the water cycle is upended.

Then, in the fall of 2003, Gadbois received a phone call. A landowner near the mouth of the Akolkolex River south of Revelstoke had brought cattle in to graze on the reed canary grass. One day in the spring, he noticed a dark and decidedly different animal grazing among his cattle: a grizzly bear, sitting peacefully, munching on fresh shoots of grass, unfazed by the other animals in his midst. More sightings of grizzly bears followed. The effect of planting the tiny, hair-like seeds had reverberated up the system to the top predators.

For Brian, it had been a resounding success.

* * *

With all of the long-planned hydro-electric projects completed, BC Hydro found itself in a new era, one unanticipated by the CRT pioneers. The corporation had thrived as a competent builder of dams, incredibly efficient with construction, completion and operation. Yet the agency was insensitive to the social and ecological turmoil its projects had caused. It was time to manage the unnatural system the CRT had created, and that included responding to public concerns about unfulfilled promises, negative consequences of reservoir life and ongoing ecological issues that kept popping up. In the late-1970s, BC Hydro began to release for sale many parcels of land that had been expropriated but not, in the end, required. They likely did not anticipate the way this release would stir once again the old regional resentments. The original swath expropriated from landowners in the 1960s all around the perimeter of the valley – from the "safe line" of 1,460 feet (445 metres) on down – had over time proven to be far more land than was necessary. BC Hydro had claimed at the time that the extra margins of land they originally took accounted for possible instability of the soil, but many local people had seen the expropriation in the 1960s as a land grab. The crown corporation's release of the land for profitable sale a decade or more later seemed to confirm those original suspicions.[9]

---

[9] Janet Spicer, personal communication, July 2007.

Some local people bought parcels of this land to make use of its resources. Others purchased pieces for recreation, or, in a few cases, reparation.[10] Others simply complained bitterly about Hydro and land-profiteering.

***

Brian retired from BC Hydro three years after I interviewed him. He began to spending more and more time on land he owns on Revelstoke Reach, the remains of an old, expropriated farm released for sale by BC Hydro in the 1980s. The former owner, Roy Nichol, had acquired the riverfront farmland in the late 1940s through a government-sponsored program that gave war veterans grants and support to do so. He had farmed it for about 20 years before the Arrow reservoir flooded him out. Brian is in the process of salvaging and restoring the remains of the old orchard above the high water mark. He has built a cabin on the property. From his vantage point on the old Nichol farm, Gadbois has a close-up view of the area that he once "farmed" as a part of the Dust Control Program.

The year after Gadbois retired, BC Hydro phased out the Dust Control Program. They justified this by pointing to the clear air and the lack of exposed, bare silt in winter months now. In the

---

[10] Janet Spicer also bid successfully on a 107-acre parcel at West Arrow Park, today served by a cable ferry. She did not intend to grow vegetables on the whole of the property; much of it was too rocky. But the purchase gave her access to the most arable land nearest the water and to a creek for irrigation. For a number of years, she grew warm weather crops: garlic, onion, potatoes, cabbage, Brussels sprouts, rutabagas, squash and beets. Technically, the fields where she planted are below the "safe line" for potential flooding in a high water year, but, she says, BC Hydro has never brought the water nearly that high in the five decades that it has operated the reservoir.

end, the program was not about ecological restoration; it was about fixing a public relations problem. After the low water years of the early 2000s – the heyday of ryegrass planting, when drought conditions and low inflows south of the border led to more water being drained from the Canadian portion of the system – the mean reservoir levels have gradually risen again. In addition, the Arrow Lakes Generating Station added to the Keenleyside Dam in 2000 now produces power most effectively when reservoir levels are relatively stable and moderately high. As much as it can within the dictates of the CRT, BC Hydro attempts to manage the reservoir levels to accommodate the power generation at Keenleyside. Weather has produced a cluster of more big water years that have also kept river levels higher. For all these reasons, the areas exposed in winter have grown smaller in the past decade. The natural influx of indigenous and some invasive species have grown to meet the planted ryegrass. The dust lands appear to be stable.

Gadbois believes cancelling the program may well have been premature. It took about 15 years after the reservoir flooded before dust was a really big problem, he says. Just as the reservoir's terrain gradually deteriorated after the construction of High Arrow, if it is left uncared for now, it may gradually revert to the condition it was in before the Dust Control Program. Small areas all along the Revelstoke Reach are still unplanted and unprotected from erosion. Without an ongoing program of planting and renewal, he fears that all the gains made over the past 20 years could be lost.

BC Hydro has installed a camera to monitor the area and watch for signs of erosion or exposure that could lead back to problems with dust. The corporation is watchful but not interested in spending any money where it doesn't absolutely have to.

Ecosystem restoration has been called a "participatory science," one that involves human beings as part of the solution, just as they have often been part of the problem. Gadbois is certain of the necessity of that approach. "The efforts have to be active and ongoing," he told me recently. "Or we may lose what we've gained." He remains actively engaged in observing and analyzing the long-term effects of the storage reservoir system and its impact.

In *The Tree of Meaning*, Canadian poet and typographer Robert Bringhurst suggests that "those who grow up, as most of us have, in industrialized economies and colonial regimes" see no other choice but to control and manage the planet's natural resources and rhythms. Bringhurst argues not for control but for participation in the relevant ecologies where we live. Those cultures that participate, he says, have learned enough about the biosphere to know that they can never be in charge. North America has a model for participatory approaches. Since long before European Contact, the practices and protocols of indigenous people did not control nature; they worked with its natural rhythms. They enhanced it and coaxed forth the best that nature could offer. In traditional Columbia River tribal cultures, people stayed in close, prayerful relationship with the non-human systems that fed and provided for them.[11] They offered gratitude for what came.

---

[11] Nadia Joe, First Nations Fisheries Council, webinar sponsored by the Polis Project, December 1, 2014.

2. Opening the Gates

As I follow the sinuous road adjacent to the north arm of Kootenay Lake, I watch the lake's water spread deep blue and endlessly north like an inland ocean. It does appear on the surface to be a damaged ecosystem, though CRT history has well taught me that appearances can be deceiving. Kootenay Lake was once a natural lake. Since the CRT, however, its natural function has been converted in subtle ways to that of a reservoir, holding water as it cycles through the Duncan and Libby dams,[1] then releasing it to travel down the West Arm and lower Kootenay River to greet the Columbia.

Did the wild grandeur and sheer size of the upper Columbia basin give political leaders in the 1950s and '60s a sense that nothing created by human beings could actually be big enough to do any significant harm? Or was the persistent, rational march of water development in the American West so unstoppable as to quickly overwhelm any intuition, any suspicion that the projects could destroy ecological health? Certainly, by the 1960s, the seeming innocence and raw idealism about industrial development

---

[1] According to BC fish biologist Jeff Burrows, the Kootenay Lake system replaces its water entirely every two years. (Personal communication, December 2014.)

expressed in the days of the Grand Coulee project had begun to wear off slightly. Enough evidence had come in that waterways with dams were adversely affected. The size of the project related directly to the size of the harm. At the heart of the problem was the heart of the river – an aquatic habitat so important to survival of fish who had evolved over millions of years. Their evolution was shaped by water that moved. In doing so, the water transferred its riches generously over hundreds and thousands of miles.

Museum archives in the upper Columbia region overflow with old black-and-white photos that record the gleeful wonder of what colonial settlers in the region found here during the first century and a half after contact: waterways brimming with big fish, little fish and all the sizes in between. On the Columbia River main stem, and on the Slocan River and Lake, Kootenay River and Lake, and Pend-d'Oreille and Lake Pend-d'Oreille systems, there seemed to be no bottom to the abundance of the fishery. Line after line pulled up another prize: trout, freshwater salmon, sturgeon. On the north end of Kootenay Lake, the Gerrard rainbow emerged from its spawning grounds in the Lardeau and Duncan valleys, a trophy fish and distant freshwater relation to the Columbia's steelhead. Today's old-timers tell stories of coolers packed annually in the 1960s with delicious burbot that spawned at the mouth of the West Arm before Duncan and Libby dams were completed upstream; of children gathering crayfish and freshwater mussels from the shores of Kootenay Lake. Of whitefish, rainbow trout, Gerrard rainbow and bull trout. It appeared as if all the fish in the world were available for anyone who had the time to throw in a line.

The migratory wonders of the past have been dealt many blows over the years. These native fisheries first felt the brunt of human industrial intervention: logging and mining. As if to gaff the fish once they had been landed, the dams stunned the natural system further. Today, in the upper Columbia region, native fisheries survive in measurable numbers in large part due to management and mitigation projects, some on a grand scale, some more local.

A program coordinated by BC Hydro to transfer bull trout around Duncan Dam is one of the latter. I've been invited to witness the manual opening and closing of the discharge gates that allow the fish to migrate to spawning grounds upstream of the dam. Few people are aware of the program, despite its interesting history, longevity and relative success. Like Brian Gadbois's work on dust control, the bull trout transfer program demonstrates how much of a difference one person can make.

⁎⁎⁎

In 1956, the US amended its Fish and Wildlife Coordination Act to place a statutory obligation on all federal projects to mitigate the effects of dams on fish and wildlife. In 1962, the US motivated the formation of a joint binational committee to address specific mitigation for Libby Dam. This committee was at first supported in BC only by regional rod and gun clubs, who lobbied the provincial government to join in. In 1963, the Libby Project Planning Committee released a report assessing Libby Dam's environmental impact in the entire Kootenay River basin. The report detailed how Libby's operation would destroy over 40,000 acres of prime winter grazing lands in the valley bottom for thousands of elk, bighorn sheep and white-tailed deer. The dam would also dry out wetlands and threaten, if not eradicate, the livelihood of prized fish, including cutthroat trout and bull trout. In 1964, the US Fish and Wildlife

Coordination Act was amended again. As Libby was being planned and constructed, environmental laws in the US were also being updated to match growing public concern.[2]

In Canada, the development of legislation to protect wild resources moved at a much slower pace. During the 1961 water licence hearings for the High Arrow project, Robert Hume of the West Kootenay Rod and Gun Club Association referred to the 1944 reference letter from both the US and Canada in which the IJC was asked to consider fish and wildlife issues in studying how to manage a dammed upper Columbia River system. Hume also quoted from transcripts of a meeting back in 1960,[3] when General McNaughton was asked about potential harm to fish and game. McNaughton had replied that the commission had not yet reached that point in its own studies. "It is a shocking thing," Hume concluded during his 1961 presentation, that in the 16 years between the reference letter and that meeting, there had been "no [federal] consideration of the impact on fish and wildlife." Finally, Hume referred to an August 1, 1961, report, "Effects on Fisheries of Four Dams Proposed for the Columbia and Kootenay Rivers in British Columbia," by F.P. Maher of the BC Fish and Wildlife Branch, and accused the provincial government of suppressing the contents of the report.[4] Paget admitted that he did not have a copy of it.

---

[2] Van Huizen.

[3] The meeting referred to was a March 28, 1960, External Affairs meeting in Ottawa.

[4] Hume had acquired a copy of the report through BC MLA George Hobbs, who had been told by the director of the Fish and Wildlife Branch to keep the contents of the report from the general public.

BC Power Commission chairman Hugh Keenleyside weighed in at the same hearing, asserting that the storage dams would have a limited effect on kokanee, the freshwater sockeye salmon common to upper Columbia lakes. "The raising of the water levels, even when it is associated with an extensive drawdown, have generally been beneficial [to fish]. We don't know that this is going to be true … but at least there is some evidence from past experience that it might be true." Hume closed his own remarks to the water comptroller by asking for a more comprehensive study of wildlife and fish ecology in advance of the flooding.

No comprehensive government study or report materialized, nor did this exchange lead to any direct mitigation plans for fish losses in that part of the system. It may, however, have helped to provide some in the Duncan and Kootenay Lake valleys. To the Duncan Dam water licence, Paget attached a requirement for a two-mile-long kokanee spawning channel to be constructed at Meadow Creek, between the dam and the outflow of the Duncan River into Kootenay Lake.[5] On the south arm of Kootenay Lake, Hydro officials also enhanced a small natural lake in marshlands to mitigate a fraction of the habitat losses in the Duncan valley. This modest effort was designed to address the loss of 4,500 acres of waterfowl habitat, tens of thousands of acres of winter feeding range, and the aquatic habitat for migratory bull trout, kokanee and the Gerrard rainbow trout.

In the summer of 1968, after the Meadow Creek Spawning Channel had opened and the dam was in operation, its caretaker, a

---

[5] BC Hydro constructed the Meadow Creek Spawning Channel in 1967–68.

first-generation immigrant from Holland named Dutchy Wageningen, noticed fish swimming up the main discharge channel against the flow of water.[6] Wageningen watched them for a few days before he called BC Hydro's head office in Vancouver. "Leave them alone," his supervisor said. "They'll go away."[7]

The fish Dutchy watched were not kokanee straying from the Meadow Creek Spawning Channel; they were bull trout. Like ocean salmon, this migrating species has a high degree of fidelity to the stream where it was born. Unlike salmon, though, bull trout can spawn several times and survive up to 20 years. Some of the trout coming up the discharge tunnel had likely been born in the upper Duncan River system. They were almost certainly returning to spawn.

Dutchy had started out at the Duncan Dam site as a powder monkey, blasting cliffs and rock. He stayed on as dam caretaker after the project was completed, grazing cows on the tidy expanse of grass BC Hydro had planted on the sloping downstream face of the earthen dam. He took his job seriously, grooming the area around the dam like a park and expressing pride in the operation of the entire facility. He hung up the phone and took matters into his own hands. Over the next few weeks, he experimented with raising and lowering the double discharge gates to see if he could help the fish get where they wanted to go. He succeeded.

---

[6] The discharge rate from Duncan reservoir is three cubic metres per second (106 cubic feet per second).

[7] Len Weins, a long-time employee at Duncan Dam who knew Dutchy before he retired, shared these stories with me in 2011.

* * *

Since Dutchy first made the personal decision to raise the gates, many thousands of bull trout have been given passage, though just as many, or more, have died from the effects of dams in the upper Columbia system. Today, the bull trout is listed as threatened on the US side of the upper Columbia, under the Endangered Species Act, and blue-listed in Canada as a "species of concern" under the Species at Risk Act. All the more reason to celebrate the actions of one rather stubborn and ingenious dam caretaker.

Dutchy's program is now formally coordinated by BC Hydro and the provincial Ministry of Environment. Opening the gates at the Duncan is a scientific and precise affair, a formal act of mitigation that gives the trout passage from Kootenay Lake into the upper reaches of a wild and watery mountain valley. Until the construction of Duncan Dam, this pristine valley carried water freely south out of icefields in Canada's Glacier National Park to the north end of Kootenay Lake, draining a region of rugged, precipitous mountains, gathering glacial silt and feeding the aquatic system. Filled with cold, rocky creeks and minor rivers, the wild valley was ideal habitat for the pugnacious bull trout.

Salvelinus confluentus are keen hunters and top aquatic predators that have been known to eat ducklings, frogs and water snakes as well as smaller fish and salmon fry. They can migrate as much as 240 kilometres (150 miles), often between river basins, in search of food. While some of the smaller bull trout take up residence in a home stream and never leave, most search out other streams or lakes, returning home only to spawn. The migrating type, which is counted at the Duncan Dam through the transfer program, can be two feet long, twice as large as the resident type. During the heady days of sport fishing on Kootenay Lake in the 1940s and '50s, when effluent from the Bluebell Mine at Riondel in the north arm was feeding the aquatic system with extra nutrients, bull trout up to 90 centimetres (three feet) long frequently took the bait, though these fish, too, were unnaturally affected by industrial activity.

I arrive at the dam and follow BC Hydro's community relations officer, Mary Anne Coules, and the present-day caretaker, Len Weins, into the mechanical room that controls the discharge gates. A steady hum fills the air. We make our way down a metal ladder and access a steel catwalk that spans one of the discharge tunnels. There, 20 feet below us, standing in a shallow pool of captured Duncan River water, are several young fish biologists and staff from the provincial environment ministry and BC Hydro. They look very happy to be there.

The discharge system at the Duncan Dam has double gates. To begin the transfer, the inner gate is closed off so that no water flows out of the reservoir into the discharge tunnel. The outer gate is opened very slowly and gradually, allowing the fish waiting on the other side to move upstream toward the closed gate. Once they have, the outer gate is closed again, trapping the fish in the water-filled concrete pen between the two. We watch the technicians weigh and measure each of the trout. They are laughing and smiling as they expertly handle the slippery fish. I wonder how many of them know the story of Dutchy's unorthodox and independent efforts. Without him, the bull trout population passing freely between Kootenay Lake and the Duncan River system might have been extirpated.

***

During the construction of Libby, it was clear that something had changed in national American environmental policy since the CRT discussions began. That something was a series of important federal laws or policies beginning with the Clean Air Act (1963) and Wilderness Act (1964), followed by the creation of the Environmental Protection Agency in 1970 and the Endangered Species Act three years later. American concern for ecological health was gradually being embedded in law.[8]

Mitigation plans for Libby Dam included a hatchery to stock the reservoir with 11,300 kilograms (25,000 pounds) of indigenous cutthroat trout, a selective withdrawal system to draw water through generators from different levels of the reservoir and control downstream river temperatures, and smaller barrier dams on tributaries to stop the migration of non-game fish into the reservoir. In addition to these efforts, the federal government purchased private lands around the reservoir to serve as wildlife preserve and compensate for lost valley bottom winter grazing.[9]

Maher's 1961 fisheries report for the BC government on the predicted effects of the CRT dams, the one Hume had accused the government of suppressing, had specifically identified habitat loss in the proposed Libby reservoir, namely flooding of spawning grounds and the impact water temperature would have on fish health as the

---

[8] John Shurts, personal communication Dec. 2014. See also Samuel Hays, *Beauty, Health and Permanence* (Cambridge: Cambridge University Press, 1989).

[9] This was a controversial initiative because it took away private holdings from already impacted local residents. (Van Huizen.)

Kootenay River's flow was held back in a hot, dry summer environment. "Water temperatures from 70-85° [21 to 29 degrees Celsius] have killed rainbow trout," he wrote. "High temperatures in the main river can drive fish into cooler tributaries where adequate spawning facilities are not available." Maher pointed to the "flooding of 42 miles [68 kilometres] of superb fishing water in the main stem Kootenay River," where "large areas appear to have suitable gravel for spawning."[10] By the time the dam was under construction, the BC government's response to environmental concerns and mitigation was tepid. Other than setting aside 1,400 acres to create Kikomun Creek Provincial Park, they funded no wildlife conservation, fisheries renewal or other protective measures for the 70 kilometres (43 miles) of reservoir extending north into British Columbia.[11] The cost ratio for the entire mitigation project in the US versus Canada was 50 to 1.[12]

Meanwhile, at Meadow Creek, the spawning channel was experiencing early success. Billed as the longest artificial channel in the world, it welcomed nearly half a million fish in the fall of 1971, over twice as many as had returned in the first year of operations, four

---

[10] Maher.

[11] The Bull River hatchery, a $1.5-million facility located in Cranbrook, opened in the mid-1960s. This was a modernized version of a hatchery for cutthroat and Gerrard rainbow that had operated in Cranbrook with the help of the Rod and Gun Club since the early 1920s. (*Cranbrook Daily Townsman,* May 6 and 13, 2011.) Small regional hatcheries once existed in several places in the upper Columbia region, most of them funded by local rod and gun clubs. Today, the Bull River hatchery is operated by the Freshwater Fisheries Society of BC, a non-profit society that also operates other hatcheries around the province.

[12] Van Huizen.

years earlier. To insure high survival rates, only 175,000 of those half a million were allowed to enter the channel. Gravel was kept clean and water flow adjusted to an inviting rate. The increased numbers indicated that human-constructed habitat might even have the potential to outstrip natural systems. "To say I'm delighted is putting it mildly," said J.W. Milligan, BC Hydro's reservoir engineer.[13]

The name *kokanee* derives from the Interior Salish word *kekeni* (redfish), common to several Salish dialects, including that spoken by the Sinixt. Kokanee operate on a four-year spawning cycle identical to that of their genetic twin, the ocean sockeye.[14] Smaller in size than the sockeye, the kokanee is an important prey for both the bull trout and the Gerrard rainbow, both of which were considered at the time of Duncan's construction to be the key to a multi-million-dollar sport fishing economy on Kootenay Lake. Local fishermen call the kokanee "feed" for the larger fish.

***

The bull trout transfer program is one of the simplest, least technical and most affordable of the wide array of fish mitigation programs that exist today across the Columbia basin, from the Pacific Ocean to the headwaters of the Columbia. These mitigation efforts range all the way from hatcheries that increase populations of kokanee, rainbow trout, sturgeon, steelhead, lamprey and ocean salmon, to fish passage involving elevators, transport tanks and conventional ladders, to nutrient enhancement of water habitat at the micro-biotic level. The program at the Duncan Dam supports bull trout numbers

---

[13] Unidentified publication, found in Touchstones Nelson archival files.

[14] While kokanee and ocean sockeye are genetically identical, they cannot cross-fertilize.

simply by giving the fish access to habitat. Some years, BC Hydro has counted 400 trout. Today, the technicians count 102. Some are nearly 90 centimetres (three feet) long. All weigh between 1.4 and 7.2 kilograms (3 and 16 pounds). I watch as the measured fish are released again into the water. Immediately, they swim to the upstream side of the concrete holding area and press their bullish snouts against the wall. They gather, brownish-grey and ghost-like, waiting for access to the relative freedom of their reservoir world. I lean out over the railing, peering down to look for the speckled "Dolly Varden" flowers on their backs. The light is too dim to distinguish the brilliant bouquets that once gave this particular fish its common name.

***

US law and policy continued to evolve in a way that supported the restoration of some of the Columbia basin's many fish-bearing rivers. In 1980, the US Congress passed legislation tasking four Pacific Northwest states with developing a plan for affordable and reliable electricity in the region. The law directs federal agencies to operate and regulate federal dams in the Columbia basin "in a manner that provides equitable treatment" to fish and wildlife alongside the other purposes of the dams. It authorized the four states to form an agency to lead the planning process, known today as the Northwest Power and Conservation Council.[15] There is no equivalent agency with such independent authority in Canada.

---

[15] Five years earlier, the Federal Columbia River Transmission System Act (1975) had made Bonneville Power Administration a self-financing federal agency with a unique structure and power to fund major fish and wildlife projects that protect endangered species.

Sometime in the 1980s, Dutchy's quietly managed grassroots program caught the attention of BC Hydro biologists as the Crown corporation slowly began to increase its ecosystem efforts in response to public scrutiny. The controversy over Revelstoke Dam had resulted in construction of another spawning channel attached to the water licence, this one at Hill Creek in the Arrow Lakes valley, complete with a hatchery for bull trout and rainbow. As the second era of dam construction drew to a close, the corporation was necessarily placing more attention on management of fish and wildlife.

By the mid-1980s, however, despite the early success of the Meadow Creek Spawning Channel, the kokanee were in big trouble on Kootenay Lake. Biologists knew that the decline of the freshwater sockeye had something to do with the food cycle. Introducing mysis shrimp to the waters of the West Arm at that time was an effort to improve it. In the end, however, the shrimp preyed on the young kokanee and made matters worse. The concentration of kokanee spawning in Meadow Creek was reducing natural distribution, increasing vulnerability to operations of that channel and slowly impacting genetic diversity.[16] By 1988, with the numbers of kokanee, bull trout and Gerrard rainbow dropping like a stone, the transfer program emerged as a BC Hydro program, complete with aquatic biologists and technicians who annually measured, tagged and counted the fish.

---

[16] Prior to the construction of the dam and channel, 8 to 11 per cent of kokanee spawned in Meadow Creek, and 82 to 89 per cent in the remainder of the Lardeau-Duncan system. After dam construction, 32 to 70 per cent spawned in the channel and only 18 to 31 per cent in the rest of the system. For more on the impacts of Duncan Dam, see Nellestijn and Decker.

At some point a few years later, the explanation for declining fish became clear to biologists. All the spawning channels in the world could not provide the kokanee with a deep, blue-water habitat rich with nutrients, an aquatic world of what fisheries biologists call "pelagic productivity." Since the 1920s, researchers had gradually built up an understanding of the link between nutrient cycles and fish health. Nutrient cycles in Kootenay Lake were feeling the effects of the two dams – Duncan and Libby. The flow of silt and other sources of microscopic food was getting trapped behind the water impoundments.[17] The water – and the fish – were starving.

In 1992, with the Kootenay Lake kokanee population near complete collapse, biologists began to experiment with increasing this pelagic productivity through the addition of common nitrate and phosphate fertilizer, dispensed from a tank attached to the Kootenay Lake ferry. This attempt to return nutrients to the lake proved successful enough that the small prey for the kokanee could survive, and the increased kokanee stocks could then serve as prey for the bull trout and Gerrard rainbow. About a decade later, the nutrient program finally expanded to the Arrow Lakes system, though not without controversy.[18]

During these decades of restoration, fisheries issues in the Canadian upper Columbia region received a boost when two regional agencies were formed, sharpening the local voice and becoming a source for more provincial funding to reach the region that had provided all the CRT storage basins. In 1994, when the first of the

---

[17] Jeff Burrows, personal communication, December 2, 2014.

[18] "Fish & Wildlife Compensation Program Hears Mouthful on State of Arrow Lakes Fishery," *Arrow Lakes News,* April 7, 2014.

three 30-year lump-sum downstream benefits agreements expired, the Canadian Entitlement began to return annually to British Columbia in the form of power that could be sold or used at a profit. Concerned about social and environmental mitigation, residents of the region formed the Columbia River Treaty Committee, hoping to benefit from the redistribution of these downstream benefits, which in contemporary markets could be worth between C$100-million and C$300-million dollars annually.[19] Eventually, the provincial government endowed the Columbia Basin Trust (CBT) with a small portion of the benefits, to address the losses stemming from the CRT. Today, the CBT administers its growing fund through various programs, with the goal of repairing the impacts of the three treaty dams and Libby in Canada. Included in its mandate is environmental mitigation. The trust also manages and operates hydro-power generators attached to Arrow, Brilliant and Waneta dams. These are designed to increase power efficiency and reduce downstream gasification for fish in facilities built from the 1940s through the 1960s without sensitivity to fish issues. The financial reach of these mitigation programs is modest by comparison to the profits generated by hydro-power production across the system.

Fish passage in the region was, and still is, limited to the grassroots program developed at Duncan Dam by its first caretaker.

Another piece of good news for fish came in 1994, when BC Hydro set aside $3.2-million annually for environmental concerns, to be

---

[19] A 2000–01 power crisis in California resulted in high market prices for electricity and made the Canadian Entitlement far more profitable than the CRT authors could have ever predicted.

administered by its newly created Columbia Basin Fish and Wild-life Compensation Program.[20] That same year, Hydro added a special weir at the Duncan Dam to assist the fish in climbing the current up to the discharge tunnel. During a study not long after that, biologists radio-tagged the bull trout being transferred and found something surprising: half of them reversed back out of the reservoir through the discharge tunnel to return to Kootenay Lake or to spawning grounds at Cooper Creek, Poplar Creek and tribu-taries of Trout Lake. Bull trout, like caribou and bison, like to range for food, with this wandering behaviour demonstrating why dams have so imperilled the aquatic migratory world of the upper basin.

* * *

The light-hearted young consultants working below me bear no resemblance to the voices of history: those government or corpo-rate officials who understated or dismissed the significance of fish values during treaty negotiations; resident fishermen and wildlife advocates whose concerns fell on deaf ears; a provincial govern-ment that invested as little as possible in mitigation projects even as it profited continually from the manufacturing and sale of electric-ity. In fact, most of those people standing below me in the concrete basin of the discharge tunnel were not alive when the treaty was signed. They are – like I imagine Dutchy to have been – activated by an earnest desire to make things work.

---

[20] In 2011, in response to provincial government directives to BC Hydro to reduce costs for its ratepayers, the Nelson office of the Fish and Wildlife Compensation Program was closed. Significant staff reductions have resulted in the program being guided and administered largely by a volunteer steering committee.

With the trout weighed and tagged, it's time to open the gates. The sheer force of water built up behind the barrier means that the concrete panels must open very, very slowly. I watch as Len removes the padlocks from the dials and turns them to open the gate a few centimetres. Water rushes noisily into the discharge tunnel through the small crack. Len explains that he will leave the water to equalize and then will return in several minutes to adjust the dial minutely. Over the next few hours, the gate will be lifted little by little. The water pressure will equalize and the bull trout will eventually find their way up into the reservoir. From that point, it will be up to them to find their natal stream, or simply search for a new food source, somewhere deep in reservoir country.[21]

As I drive south again, I think about the handsome bull trout caught up in the arms of the young fish biologists and technicians, and about Richard Welton's testimony at the water licence hearings. Welton's description of the flow of nutrients from the Duncan River basin into the north arm of Kootenay Lake is one of the most vivid prizes of landscape ephemera that I have captured in my net over the past decade of research. A giant plume of nutrient-flushing took

---

[21] In the upper Columbia region, bull trout make a respectable showing in a few reservoirs. Revelstoke reservoir below Mica Dam, and Kinbasket reservoir above it, sustain bull trout in part because smaller prey fish are able to pass or "entrain" through the Mica turbines from Kinbasket reservoir into Revelstoke reservoir unharmed. Above Mica Dam, the water is cold enough, the prey numerous enough and the tributary spawning habitat plentiful enough that bull trout sustains a modest population without intervention. (Steve Arndt, interview by author, February 2011.) The top two tributary rivers for bull trout are the Illecillewaet (where a small dam was removed in 1985) and Incomappleux rivers, both near Revelstoke. (Jeff Burrows, interview by author, December 2014.)

place annually, without any human intervention. Nutrient transfer also took place in smaller, more frequent ways during intense precipitation events in the fall and early summer. Each time that the water surged down out of the high alpine or through a river basin or creek drainage, it carried with it minerals and decayed vegetation gathered along the way. These minerals and decaying matter formed the pelagic marvel of microscopic zooplankton and algae that drove a healthy fishery – from the bottom of the big blue water on up.[22]

The Kootenay Lake system was not directly affected by the loss of the ocean salmon from the construction of Grand Coulee, as were the Arrow and Slocan River valleys. The falls west of Nelson, BC, had already created a natural barrier, though there is plenty of evidence that at some point before the last glaciation, ocean fish did make it past the natural impediments on the lower Kootenay River. Removal of ocean nutrients is, however, an important factor in the overall decline of the aquatic system in the upper basin. Salmon, when they spawn and die, provide a rich source of food to river systems and forests. The completion of Grand Coulee Dam caused a cascade of losses both for terrestrial species and for the health of the water on the Columbia's main stem and all its tributaries.

While their successes are small in the face of the many harmful impacts of dams, the bull trout transfer and ryegrass programs both feel like gestures of positive human potential to participate in

---

[22] Two major sources of industrial effluent had an ironically positive influence on the Kootenay Lake fishery in the 20th century by feeding the micro-nutrient system inadvertently: the Bluebell Mine on the North Arm of Kootenay Lake from 1950 to 1972, and Crestbrook Forest Industries upstream near Cranbrook from 1975 to the 1990s.

the closing of a circle. These programs model direct, conciliatory engagement with natural systems that have been deeply harmed by corporate water development. The two open ends of that circle represent two versions of use in the region: pre-Contact indigenous sustainability on the one hand and intense colonial resource extraction on the other. These two versions remain largely separate in the contemporary mind, with indigenous sustainability often seen as a nostalgic but unrealistic option and dams with affordable hydroelectricity a necessity that justifies the damage they have done. The space between these two extremes may close slowly. That process is limited by cultural reluctance to value mitigation projects more, by misunderstandings and unhealed wounds, and by an industrial system that has few protocols for sustainable respect and honour of resource use. But close the circle we must if the region's aquatic ecosystem is to recover any of its former richness and resilience.

The fish, the water and the land are not, as they once seemed to the treaty authors, infinitely abundant or resilient. They need care and support to grow strong again. How can a renewed CRT help restore the once dynamic and now deeply damaged landscape and water of the upper Columbia basin? The current approach of BC Hydro and the provincial government can at best be defined as complacent. The official response focuses on pulling fisheries back from a cliff of complete collapse, but not on cultivating or funding an atmosphere of stewardship. The limited programs in place risk being downsized or eliminated by socio-economic factors.[23]

This is not just a regional challenge. It represents the challenge facing all of us, wherever we live, to experience a more sustainable,

---

[23] Nellestijn and Decker.

more reciprocal and more grateful relationship with the places where we live. How much do we take from the place we call home? How much do we give back? Linking mitigation efforts directly to a redesign of the CRT would entrench a broader set of more sustainable values in its framework. Keenleyside's unsubstantiated theory about the reservoir not harming fish has been firmly rebutted by 50 years of aquatic loss. It is important to recognize what history has taught us through the lens of hindsight and to continue the learning: the era of rationalization that began with the negotiation and formation of the CRT may not be over.

***

Sinixt fishermen once fished for the bull trout in the region's streams by trolling with a hook made from a shard of deer shin bone, bound with sinew to a fishing line of twisted hemp. They baited the hook with salmon eggs or small fish. Often, a fisherman would troll from the shore by walking upstream along the riverbank, holding the line in his teeth to better feel the bite. His relationship with place was direct, elemental and respectful. The bull trout he sought was emblematic of the many rocky streams threading through imposing, ice-capped mountains in the traditional territory of this indigenous tribe, so much so that they took their very name from the fish: *Sin* (people in the place of) *ixt* (the bull trout). A fish that wants and deserves the freedom to roam; a ranging, hungry keystone of the upper Columbia system. A fisherman, grateful for the miracle of a cold mountain stream.

3. The Voice of the Grandmothers

Early on in this project, something wild in me woke up to the sound of water. A boulder makes a particular noise when a raucous snow-melt stream pushes it along. *Thwoooo-ump*. And then again, a few minutes later: *Thwoooo-ump*.

This is the sound of strength and flexibility.

Once awakened, I drove far to see what happened to water once it was dammed. As consolation, I camped beside free-running water whenever I could, to listen. The emotional value of the water hit me hard: anger, suppression, defiance and survival. Excitement, calm, urgency and ooze. Water, I discovered, is large and miraculous.

Though I am wounded and wiser now than when I began this journey through the history of the Columbia River Treaty, I press on. It's important to close the circle on my research.

* * *

Hart Lake is located on private land within the Colville National Forest, about eight kilometres (five miles) south of the international boundary as the crow flies. The sky threatens rain as a group of modern-day Sinixt basket-weavers drives upstream from Kettle Falls, Washington, following the Kettle River drainage, a tributary of the Columbia. This is the river their ancestors called Nehoial-pitku.[1] Well beyond Orient, Washington, we turn onto a side road and climb a gentle range of mountains rising between the Columbia and Kettle River valleys. Today, the Sinixt people call this rolling, rocky terrain Kelly Hill. Many have allotments here, dating back to the time when the "north half" of their American reservation was opened to settlers. We turn down a gravel road and pull up beside Hart Lake. Tules are growing at the shoreline; we have come to gather some. Since the 1990s, Hart Lake has increased from 5 acres to over 20, largely as a result of beavers being allowed to build dams at its outlet. Some parts of the spring-fed lake are over 15 metres (50 feet) deep. Much of the more recent water is shallow, forming an ideal habitat for the tule (*Schoenoplectus acutus*) to thrive. The Sinixt call the giant, thick-stemmed plants *tekwatan*. It has been used for thousands of years by many tribes in many places along the Columbia and throughout the northwest to fabricate mats, roofs and floor coverings, as well as other household items. The Sinixt made waterproof mats from tule to cover their summer travelling shelters, their salmon-drying racks at Sounding Waters and the floors of their winter lodges, among other uses. Before Grand Cou-lee Dam, they would find the tule in the sloughs and shallow water areas along the shores of the Columbia River. Some tribes – includ-ing the Wanapum on the Columbia and the Pomo in northern

---

[1] No confirmed translation of the word's meaning exists.

California – once made entire houses out of the grass. Others – the Bay Miwok, Coast Miwok and Ohlone of California – bundled and sewed them into canoes. The Nahuati (California) tribal name for the plant, *tollin*, forms the root of *tule*, the English word most tribes use today.[2]

We stop, unload and form a circle. Before we begin, a prayer of gratitude takes the form of a song, sung by one of the gatherers. The voice floats across the water of Hart Lake and rubs up against a forested slope on the other side. There is no room for any other sound. When the song is over, the world feels larger, more welcoming and receptive to our work.

I pull out my hip waders. Someone gives me a knife. My hands reach deep into the water, searching for the base of the plant's stem. A few tules pop up after a gentle tug and twist by hand, others take slicing. The stems are long and lightweight, cool and slippery in my hands. Some are seven feet tall, reaching toward the sky. I wander further from shore, stepping deeper into the juicy mud, searching for the ideal strands – plump, unblemished and straight. Soon I am into Hart Lake up to my waist.

---

[2] Turner, Bouchard and Kennedy; Wikipedia, "tule." A few more magical uses of this water-borne plant bear mentioning. In 1850, the US Cavalry surrounded and killed most of a group of Pomo Indians gathered at Clear Lake in northern California to harvest spring-spawning fish. One of the only survivors of the Bloody Island Massacre, 6-year-old Ni'ka, or Lucy Moore, evaded notice by hiding underwater and using a tule stem as a breathing tube. In the upper Columbia region, stems were woven into mats that swelled when wet, increasing their ability to repel rain. They were also commonly used to make headdresses for Lakes and Skoyelpi healers, known by many as "Indian doctors" or "shamans."

In just a few hours, the work of gathering is finished. We tie the bundles and wrap them in clean sheets. We load them carefully into the truck and head back to the reservation, where we lay the *tekwatan* out to dry, for use on another day.

We turn to cedar bark basket-weaving. We change into dry clothes, fill mugs with tea, and settle in around the table. I tell the story of bringing my "Canadian" cedar bark across the day before.

You can't bring bark across, the border agent said. *Unless it's varnished.* She frowned as she cited the federal order banning the import of firewood. I listened but said nothing. I could tell she wanted to let me go across. She spoke again: *Native Americans can bring baskets, hides, eagle feathers and otherwise prohibited items from Canada into the US, but only if they are used for religious and ceremonial purposes.* She paused, studying my face. *Are you an Indian?*

I shook my head.

Laughter erupts in the weaving circle. *Dead bark is illegal now?* More laughter. *First us Lakes people can't cross the border to be on our land, to get our berries and our meat. Now it's our bark that can't cross.* More laughter. When it subsides, I explain how the agent eventually let me across, after extracting a promise to bring my bark and the newly made basket straight back to Canada the next day.

More than a decade after I harvested the bark, near Kaslo, BC, the cedar emerges from the soaking basin as if I had pulled it yesterday from a tree.[3] The air is fresh with the scent of awakened sap as my fingers struggle to master the simple technique. I have worked with yarn, thread, wire, cord and fabric, but never with the fibres of a tree.

---

[3] For more on the harvest and many uses of cedar bark and roots, see Stewart.

At first, I weave the honey-brown, flexible strips in a clumsy way. The strength and patience of the tree gradually expands between my fingers, calling me back into the upper Columbia forests, where one of the West's greatest rivers begins. One strip that I take from the water bath is too thick to weave. I am taught how to split the fibres. Using my thumbs and index fingers, I search for a natural parting in them and follow it just like I would separate a stack of paper or a pair of chewing gum sticks. One flat, thick strip soon becomes two that are more pliable.

As my fingers guide the fibres to be sure they divide evenly, I think of the accumulated years that form dense layers in any life. Years of heavy rain, of drought or extreme cold. Years when the wind blew hard against the branches. Years when the salmon ran over the falls with profusion. Years when a mother eagle screeched protectively in the tree's crown. Time peels away as I work. Around me, the Sinixt basket-weavers chatter and laugh. They share stories, tease each other and support with humour the patience this task requires. Memories inside of me ready themselves to be loosened and removed. The walls of my small basket slowly grow taller.

One of the weavers is related through marriage to an old Indian lady I learned of during my research named Able-One. The weaver never knew Able-One, of course. Nor did I. Able-One would be 200 years old if alive today. But Able-One told many stories in the old way of her people. And, thank goodness, Able-One's granddaughter Nancy wrote down everything her grandmother told her. I came across Able-One's story in an elegant, inspiring and privately published memoir, *In the Stream*.[4] The weaver remembers Able-

---

[4] A link to a PDF of this book can be found at http://tina.nichebox.com.

One's granddaughter Nancy's own daughter, the weaver's auntie-in-law, who died only a few years ago, in her early 90s. The weaver knows all about Able-One, one of the family's esteemed ancestral grandmothers.

I have been gently woven into the circle of Indian women around me. They are so much like me, yet so different. They are full of laughter and acceptance. They are from this place, they belong here. They enclose me in a story I have not heard before, a feminine story of the Columbia River, one that moves beyond borders as I guide the cedar strips back and forth – passing them between the landscape of their origin and my working hands.

* * *

Able-One was born in a village on the shores of the Columbia River in about 1815, at the start of a ceremony that the Sinixt called the Song of Fruitage. The river was coming alive again after winter silence and the plants were giving green shoots when Able-One arrived, beside a traditional women's bathing pool warmed with hot stones. After the birth, she was washed and oiled, then wrapped in soft skins well padded with the down of cattail and laced into a snug sack. Her birth kept Able-One's mother from participating in the traditional ceremonies as wife of a Sinixt chief named With-ered-Top. She could only watch as the women danced past her near the water. The chief's wife held her baby daughter aloft, listening to the song. *Let the bow bend with fruit and the ground heave up with roots.* Able-One's mother next waved her digging stick high in the air over her head. The women danced on. *That our bark baskets may overflow and the supplies might flow through our hand.*

In the following days, the women cleansed themselves carefully in preparation for gathering and processing the plant foods: "The pools hissed and bubbled, throwing steam in the clean, sparkling air. With a short paddle, red-hot stones were thrown together with a measure of clean ashes ... turning the water a smoky color while the next pool was bailed out and refilled with clear water and tempered with a stone or two. The bathers would step down into the first pool and bathe, and then step to the clean pool before drying before the fire."

One day when Able-One was a little girl, her mother noticed her fear of water. She asked for the chief's permission to use the men's fishing platform, suspended over a small waterfall. He agreed. That evening, Able-One's mother led her out onto the platform along the ladder of braided willow bark. Being afraid of water, she said, was like being afraid of a good friend. She left Able-One there and retreated, removing the cross bars from the ladder as she went.

Stranded over the active current, unaware that several men kept close watch on the shore, Able-One clung to the swaying platform, closing her eyes and moaning as darkness fell. Much to her surprise, the currents below her eventually began to sing and laugh. She grew comfortable enough to sleep. In her dreams, she was thrown from the platform into the water, where she found a large shellfish on the stream bed. *Do as I do,* the creature said. *Go to the bottom and walk out.* Able-One awoke perfectly dry, swinging gently and safely on the platform. Dawn came. Her mother returned and found her daughter cured of her fear of the water.

The Columbia's annual spring flood once found many soft alluvial pockets along the shore. Able-One recalled how the water "receded from the banks and the rich sediment provided a place where camas grew large and shallow." Women dug the bulbs of

Camassia quamash, cooked them in pits and stored them for winter. They picked wild strawberries, soopolalli berries, huckleberries and rosehips, drying them on tule mats and pressing them into cakes. They cut and dried salmon on racks shielded from summer rain by woven tule mats. They cooked, pounded and dried the wild game, prepared their skins, rendered their fat. They washed animal intestines in river water and stuffed them with berries, meat and fat.

When the time of low water arrived in autumn, long lines of Sinixt people made their way to the shores of the Columbia, where they loaded their laden food bags into canoes and paddled upstream to winter villages where they would be protected from fierce wind and have good winter sun. On one such autumn journey, when Able-One was still a young girl, she travelled with her father, Chief Withered-Top, who had been blinded recently by one of the measles epidemics, and her mother, nine months pregnant. At one point, her mother abruptly steered the canoe into a sandy cove, grasped a branch from a willow growing on the shore, and gave it to her husband to hold before disappearing over the top of the riverbank into the forest. It seemed a long time before Able-One heard her mother's voice again. *We have received a man in our midst*, her mother called out, coming slowly down the steep bank with the baby wrapped in her deerskin skirt. She washed the newborn in the river and swaddled him tightly.

As an old woman sitting by the winter fire many years later, Able-One described river water to her granddaughter Nancy, who listened very carefully. The river was *the essence of life, a place of mystery and power that was at once teacher and friend*. Able-One recalled to her granddaughter how one day, just before her adolescence, she was trained by and invited into the circle of women. Her mother took her down to the river and explained that a person who follows and adheres to the traditions of the people will disperse back into the stream when he or she dies. This, her mother said, was called keeping the Lakes way. At that moment, the girls and young women of the village emerged from the shadows where they had been watching. Surrounding Able-One in a circular embrace, they moved along the shore of the Columbia chanting in low voices. Able-One watched as the women dipped their hands in the river, passed them over their sense organs and sang.

Carry us in the centre of the stream of life, where we shall never waste but enlarge and deepen thy strength.

* * *

I return to Canada with an unfinished basket sitting on the passenger seat beside me. One of the most experienced weavers had noticed as the day of weaving drew to a close that I was rushing to finish. *The process shouldn't be rushed* she told me, laying a hand gently on the basket. *I know you want to take it home finished. Next time. You have begun a lovely first basket. Let's make it right, to the end.*

So often, the rush to finish gets in the way. We get an idea. To build something, maybe. To make a big change. We are proud and excited. We start working and can't believe we have figured it out. We can't believe what a great idea it is, how well it is going, at first. We are so excited that we press ourselves to finish. In the flurry and willfulness of it all, in the rush to complete what we started, so that we can be even more proud of our idea and how well it works, we lose hold of something important.

We stop listening to the basket. We stop listening to the river. We stop listening to the Earth that is our home.

***

The following spring, I travel to Portland, Oregon, to participate in a conference on salmon restoration sponsored by the 15 united tribes living along the "American" portion of the Columbia River. Early in the morning on day two of the conference, Charlotte Rodrique, chairperson and elder of the Burns Paiute Tribe of central Oregon, speaks about water.

I'm an old-time Indian woman, she begins. The room, filled with tribal men, immediately goes quiet. She continues.

I feel uncomfortable speaking in public.

Her voice is soft but every word is clear, well-thought. All the breakfast and tinkling coffee sounds in the room have disappeared. I reach for my notebook.

It was never our people's way for the women to speak out. That was for the men. When the men spoke, the grandmothers were there, but they were standing behind them. They were reminding them of who they were. I will give it a try.

The banquet room feels as quiet and large and beautiful as the world was that day beside Hart Lake. Charlotte Rodrique goes on, telling a story of going with her grandmother many years ago to gather plant medicine high in the mountains above the Snake River. Her grandmother at one point asked her to get water, explaining how to carefully part the lichen and moss gathered around the springs emerging from the ground. She told her granddaughter to be so very careful with the water, not to harm it. Water was precious, her grandmother told her.

Rodrique is a woman of small stature, in possession of a pair of dark brown eyes that glisten like a river-swell on a sunny, bright day.

Water is what we pray with, she says. *We dip eagle feathers in water and brush people with it when they are sick. It helps them heal.* She concludes by reminding everyone in the room – the tribal leaders, fish biologists, legal experts, hydro-industry representatives and government consultants – that she will be the grandmother behind their backs. *We need to leave the river better than it was before. We need to support each other in this work. Please don't forget.*

On the flight back to Spokane, I have a window seat. The sky is perfectly clear. Far below me, the Channeled Scablands, formed by the glacial flood from ancient Lake Missoula, ripple like water. The tightly managed Columbia River cuts cleanly through the ancient, undulating silt, though from up this high, I feel and sense something still wild in the river. I can't take my eyes off the grandeur of it all – the landscape's expansive, lively form illuminated by a late afternoon sun, and the miraculous, blue slice of a river finding its way. The river still moves in a few places. This gives me hope.

I crane my neck to see as much as I can out the tiny airplane window. The history of the Columbia River Treaty began with an optimism, certainty and accomplishment that was quickly diluted by political egos, betrayal and disagreement. This history speaks a universal message of cultural habits many of us have inherited: we think about the future without knowing the past; we take without measure; we overlook the practice of gratitude. We talk more than we listen; we argue; we are in such a big hurry. It's hard, or nearly impossible, to hear and feel the true desire of the water over the clamour of our voices. Over industry's rational focus on profits for shareholders, on what we have all come to think of as economic stability and on a hope for prosperity. Over the second- and third-generation farmers, thirsty for more water, anxious to have all that they need. Over the judgment implicit in the environmentalists, who urge the protection of wild places and the cleaning up of the water, and often speak with blame. Even the most recent, scientifically noble warnings and concerns about climate change are not immune to the clamour. Some of those who find themselves rightly concerned about the impact of climate change in the Columbia River watershed have recently advocated for more storage reservoirs to be constructed, and for the CRT storage reservoirs in Canada to stay full to the brim. As the theory goes, they want to hold back the cold mountain water so that it can charge the system, to salvage in an unnatural way some of the cool temperatures that were always the river's birthright. The Columbia River will only grow warmer and dryer with the doomed predictions of big changes in the climate, they say. These plans ignore the deep ecological damage that large storage reservoirs inflict on landscape. They ignore the call of a wild river that is tired of being told what to do.

My heart always sinks whenever I hear another version of the future being proposed alongside another theory about what to do. *As the theory goes.* We thought we knew best in the 1950s and '60s. Were we right then? Is there any way around our powerful human ability to rationalize, theorize and control the river? The possibility of renegotiation or renewal of the CRT has appeared on the horizon. It's important to remember, however, that the treaty has no expiration. This treaty is a forever deal, unless either country speaks up. It is my hope that those engaged in discussions will remember that it is impossible to know the present or to explore future possibilities without understanding well the terrain of the past.

. We will need a tightly woven basket to hold all our clamouring voices, all our opinions and theories about how to best use the

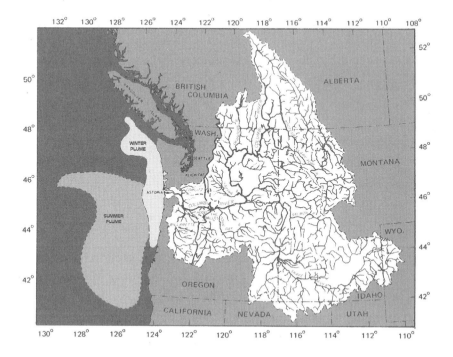

This map of the Columbia basin illustrates the dense network of tributaries that feed the main stem of the Columbia, as well as the (contemporary) spread of summer and winter outflows into the Pacific

precious water held by the Columbia River, for *our* purposes or to support *our* theories. This basket must also be large enough to give us space to listen to each other. But perhaps most important, we will need a basket woven to hold the miraculous sound that free-running water makes.

Let's not forget to ask what the river wants. Or what it needs.

Acknowledgments

Many generous people line the challenging road through Columbia River Treaty history.

Thanks in particular to those who took time to share personal stories of betrayal and loss: Mary Bajowsky, Brian Gadbois, Larry Greenlaw, Brenda Buerge, and Crystal and Janet Spicer. I also honour Stan Triggs, who climbed into a rowboat, saw and remembered.

Touchstones Nelson Museum of Art and History asked me to curate an exhibit on the Columbia River Treaty in 2015, work that influenced the shape and direction of this project. Thanks to executive director Leah Best and archivist Laura Fortier, for your support.

Kelvin Ketchum, Doug Robinson and Alan Thomson provided expertise in water engineering, treaty history and how natural rivers work. I thank them for enduring my questions.

For sharing resources, enthusiasm and time: Patti Bailey, Virgil Seymour and other Arrow Lakes tribal members, the Deane family, Catherine Fischer, Alistair and Dorothy Fraser, John Harrison,

Anne Irving, Greg Nesteroff, Jack Nisbet, Ron and Francis Welwood, and Kyle Kusch of the Arrow Lakes Historical Society.

Of the many print and archival materials I consulted, I owe a particular debt to the scholarship of Neil Swainson, Donald Waterfield, Dorothy Kennedy and Randy Bouchard. Tina Wynecoop, librarian and friend, shared many resources, and offered constant faith in the river and its story. Don Gorman at Rocky Mountain Books and his talented copy-editor Peter Norman have helped me carry the book on its final run into the world.

To Yasodhara Ashram, my sisters Nancy and Nora, George and Jack Pearkes, and extended family: you are my bedrock.

Bibliography

Arnold, Laurie. *Bartering with the Bones of Their Dead: The Colville Confederated Tribes and Termination.* Seattle: University of Washington Press, 2012.

Baynes Lake Senior Book Club. *South Country History Book: A Valley Remembered.* Baynes Lake: Baynes Lake Senior Book Club, 2007.

BC Environment & Lake Use Committee. *Mica Reservoir Region Resource Study: Final Report.* 1974.

Berry, Wendell. *Life is a Miracle.* Washington, DC: Counterpoint, 2000.

Bouchard, Randy, and Dorothy Kennedy. *First Nations' Ethnography and Ethnohistory in British Columbia's Lower Kootenay Columbia Hydropower Region.* 2000. Reprint, Castlegar, BC: Columbia Power, 2003.

———. "Indian Land Use and Occupancy in the Franklin D. Roosevelt Lake Area of Washington State". Final report for the Colville Federated Tribes and the United States Bureau of Reclamation. BC Indian Language Project, Victoria, BC, 1984.

———. "Utilization of Fish by the Colville Okanagan Indian People" (unpublished manuscript, BC Indian Language Project, Victoria, BC, 1975).

Bringhurst, Robert. *The Tree of Meaning: Language, Mind and Ecology*. Berkeley, CA: Counterpoint, 2007.

Brogan, Chris. "The Hudson's Bay Company and Native Salmon: Subsistence Security during the Early Years of the Colville District, 1821–31" (unpublished manuscript).

Chance, David. *People of the Falls*. Kettle Falls: Kettle Falls Historical Center, 1986.

Collier, Donald, Alfred E. Hudson and Arlo Ford. "Archaeology of the Upper Columbia Region." University of Washington Publications in Anthropology, vol. 9, no. 1. Seattle: University of Washington Press, 1942.

Corner, John. *Pictographs in the Interior of British Columbia*. Vernon, BC: 1968.

Darland, Alvin F. "A Brief Chronological History of the Construction of Grand Coulee Dam," from *Pioneers to Power*, 1958.

Douglas, David. *Journal kept by David Douglas during His Travels in North America 1823–1827*. London: W. Wesley & Son, 1914.

Duff, Wilson. *The Indian History of British Columbia: The Impact of the White Man*. Victoria: Royal British Columbia Museum, 1997.

Jenish, D'Arcy. *Epic Wanderer: David Thompson and the Mapping of the Canadian West*. Toronto: Anchor Canada, 2004.

Galm, Jerry, ed. *A Design for Management of Cultural Resources in the Lake Roosevelt Basin of Northeastern Washington*. Cheney: Eastern Washington University Reports in Archaeology and History, 1994.

Geiger, Andrea. "Crossed by the Border: The U.S.–Canada Border and Canada's 'Extinction' of the Arrow Lakes Band, 1890–1956." *Western Legal History* 23, no. 2 (2010).

Graham, Clara. *This Was the Kootenay*. Vancouver: Evergreen Press, 1963.

Havdale, Daisy. *The Lost Valley*. Victoria, 2010.

Holmes, Richard. *The Age of Wonder: How the Romantic Generation Discovered the Beauty and Terror of Science*. London: HarperCollins, 2008.

Hyde, Lewis. *The Gift: Creativity and the Artist in the Modern World*. 2nd Vintage Books ed. New York: Vintage Books, 2007.

International Joint Commission. *Report of the International Joint Commission, United States and Canada on Principles for Determining and Apportioning Benefits from Cooperative Use of the Storage of Waters and Electrical Inter-Connection within the Columbia River System*. December 29, 1959.

Jamison, Michael. "Dead & Buried: Reflections on life before Libby Dam." *The Missoulian,* August 22, 2004. http://missoulian.com/news/state-and-regional/dead-and-buried-reflections-on-life-before-the-libby-dam/article_766ffec0-742d-56d6-bf12-7b01cda83120.html.

Krutilla, John V. *The Columbia River Treaty: The Economics of an International River Basin Development*. Baltimore: Johns Hopkins University Press, 1967.

Leighton, Caroline. *West Coast Journeys, 1865–1879: The Travelogue of a Remarkable Woman*. Seattle: Sasquatch Books, 2002.

Louie, Martin. "Tales of Coyote: Eastern Washington Traditions as told by Martin Louie, Sr.," in *A Columbia River Reader,* edited by William L. Lang. Tacoma: Washington State Historical Society, 1992.

Maher, F.P. *A Preliminary Report on the Effects on Fisheries of Four Dams Proposed for the Columbia and Kootenay Rivers in British Columbia*. Victoria: Fish & Game Branch, BC Department of Recreation & Conservation, August, 1961.

McDonald, Angus. "A Few Items of the West." *The Washington Historical Quarterly* 8, no. 3 (1917).

McDonald, Archibald. *This Blessed Wilderness: Archibald McDonald's Letters from the Columbia, 1822–44*. Edited by Jean Murray Cole. Vancouver: University of British Columbia Press, 2001.

McDonald, J.D. *Storm Over High Arrow: The Columbia River Treaty (A History)*. n.p.: Hall Printing, 1993.

Mitchell, David J. *W.A.C. Bennett and the Rise of British Columbia*. Vancouver: Douglas & McIntyre, 1983.

Mohs, Gordon. *Post-Inundation Archaeological Survey Studies of the Arrow Lakes*. Commissioned by BC Hydro, 1977.

Morgan, Murray. *The Columbia, Powerhouse of the West*. Seattle: Superior, 1949.

Morton, Val. *Dam Lies: Val Morton's Struggle with BC Hydro's Expropriation of His Family Home and Property*. Victoria, 2006.

Mouat, Jeremy. *The Business of Power: Hydro-Electricity in Southeastern British Columbia, 1897–1997*. Victoria: Sono Nis, 1997.

Nellestijn, G., and S. Decker. *Lardeau and Lower Duncan River Watershed Profile*. Prepared for the Friends of the Lardeau River, Howser, BC, 2011.

Nisbet, Jack. *Sources of the River*. Seattle: Sasquatch Books, 2011.

Simpson, Sir George. *An Overland Journey Round the World, During the Years 1841 and 1842*. Philadelphia: Lea & Blanchard, 1847.

Spritzer, Donald E. *Waters of Wealth: The Story of the Kootenai River and Libby Dam*. Boulder, CO: Pruett, 1979.

Stanley, Meg. *Voices from Two Rivers: Harnessing the Power of the Peace & Columbia Rivers*. Vancouver: Douglas & McIntyre, 2010.

Stewart, Hilary. *Cedar*. Vancouver: Douglas & McIntyre, 1995.

Swainson, Neil. *Conflict over the Columbia*. Montreal: McGill-Queen's University Press, 1979.

Swettenham, John. *McNaughton*. 3 vols. Toronto: Ryerson Press, 1968.

Turner, Nancy J. *Ancient Pathways, Ancestral Knowledge*. 2 vols. Montreal: McGill-Queen's University Press, 2014.

Turner, Nancy J., Randy Bouchard and Dorothy Kennedy. *Ethnobotany of the Okanagan–Colville Indians of B.C. and Washington*. Victoria: Royal British Columbia Museum, 1980.

US Department of the Interior. *The Columbia River: A Comprehensive Departmental Report on the Development of the Water Resources of the Columbia River Basin for Review Prior to Submission to Congress*. Washington, DC: US Department of the Interior, 1947.

Van Huizen, Philip. "Building a Green Dam: Environmental Modernism and the Canadian-American Libby Dam Project." *Pacific Historical Review* 79, no. 3 (2010).

Waterfield, Donald. *Continental Waterboy: The Columbia River Controversy*. Toronto: Clarke, Irwin, 1970.

———. *Land Grab: One Man versus the Authority*. Toronto: Clarke, Irwin, 1973.

Wedemeyer, Olga. *The Story of the Tobacco Plains Country*. Caldwell, ID: Pioneers of the Tobacco Plains Country, 1950.

White, Richard. *The Organic Machine: The Remaking of the Columbia River.* New York: Hill & Wang, 1996.

Wilson, Jim. *People in the Way: The Human Aspects of the Columbia River Project.* Toronto: University of Toronto Press, 1973.

Wynecoop, Nancy Perkins, and N. Wynecoop Clark. *In The Stream: An Indian Story.* Spokane, 1985.

Index